DEVELOPMENT OF UNIVERSITY LIBRARIES IN INDIA AFTER INDEPENDENCE

CONCEPTS IN COMMUNICATION
INFORMATICS & LIBRARIANSHIP
(CICIL)

For a list of titles in this series,
please see pp. 225 at the end of the book.

Concepts in Communication
Informatics & Librarianship-31

General Editor: **S.P. Agrawal**

DEVELOPMENT OF UNIVERSITY LIBRARIES IN INDIA AFTER INDEPENDENCE

O.P. GUPTA

CONCEPT PUBLISHING COMPANY, NEW DELHI 110059

ISBN 81-7022-409-8

First Published 1992

Published and Printed by
Ashok Kumar Mittal
Concept Publishing Company
A/15-16, Commercial Block, Mohan Garden
NEW DELHI-110059 (India)

Lasertypeset by
Microtech Advance Printing Systems (Pvt.) Ltd.
H-13, Bali Nagar
NEW DELHI-110015

GENERAL EDITOR'S INTRODUCTION

Believe it or not — it depends, but it's true that a library is very much a nerve-centre of the parent organisation and occupies a central place therein. No doubt, therefore, that a university library is one of the most effective and powerful instruments through which the university can realise its objectives. With adequate resources, the library can render useful service to the university in performance of almost all functions and activities—teaching, learning and research, creation of new knowledge, and dissemination of accumulated wisdom of the past as well as of learning and culture of the present. Like a university, the university library has also to establish relationship with the community, and through extension services endeavour to bring about social change among the people—it is particularly so for the developing world.

In the West, the universities have long recognised the importance of libraries in realisation of their goals and consequently have given top priority for library development. The university libraries there have adequate funds at their disposal and are provided with competent and suitably trained personnel, the latest gadgets and equipments as well as all the necessary infrastructure so as to be able to provide modern services to the users. But in India, scenario of the university libraries is depressingly different. The Commissions and Committees set up by Government of India from time to time have, one and all, emphasised the need for building up university libraries on modern lines to make them serve the universities in an effective way. Still most of them are a neglected lot so much so that some of these libraries fail even to provide bare minimum services to the academic community. Of course, there are university libraries, particularly libraries of the Central Universities, which have adequate resources, trained staff and the necessary information infrastructure for catering to the needs of the users, but then such libraries are far and few. Surprising indeed, even these developed libraries are unable to measure up to their counterparts in the West– still not equipped as these are with the latest information technologies and not therefore in a position to provide automative services.

University Grants Commission has been playing a dynamic role for improving the working of the university libraries through various programmes, and whatsoever improvement in the services of these libraries is noticeable is because of UGC's sustained efforts. But then what can the Commission do! In view of the phenomenal increase in number of university and college libraries, as against the limited funds made available by the Government exchequer, UGC also remains a silent spectator by and large.

Since the objectives and functions of a university library are dependent upon those of the university it serves, the present CICIL publication attempts to examine in detail the aims and objectives of higher education in the context of the changing modern world, traces the historical development of both universities and university libraries in India, and also indicates briefly the recommendations of the Committees and Commissions pertaining to library development. The main focus of the book, nonetheless, is on the role of the University Grants Commission in building up and modernising the university libraries *inter alia* detailing the quality improvement programmes, particularly of the library personnel, initiated in the light of the recommendations made by various Committees constituted by the University Grants Commission.

S.P. AGRAWAL

PREFACE

Education is a dynamic process to develop total personality. Reason of that in the end of the 20th Century, the achievement and initiatives of free democratic India's higher educational approaches are under review. Traditional growth has to be revalidated to meet future programmes. Socio-Cultural, Economic and Industrial Revolutions has close relation with Information explosion. The Information dissemination has crucial role in research and academic activities. It has become more relevant when libraries and library and information science have become a subject of regular discussion at national and international level. Even then nothing concrete has been done to improve the library services in universities and colleges.

While working in national higher education information service centre, i.e, UGC Library, I discussed the subject with librarians who have intimate knowledge of the subject. The library staff, which is a bridge between students, teachers and books, should have service standards to strengthen the relationship. Application of modern technologies to meet the faster development of information has also invited attention. Since all the service activities have direct bearing on resources and national policies, it will be helpful to review the UGC assistance and initiatives.

In last four decades UGC's high priorities for libraries has revolutionised university libraries in terms of infrastructure, collections, services and services conditions, etc. Surveys, case studies, debates, conferences, seminars have laid stress on multifarious complex activities and tremendous information explosion. The study is based on the experience, negotiations and published documents. The attempt is to bring out deliberations and resolutions in their chronological subject sequence to assess the growth.

The study is in five chapters. First chapter is Introduction history background of education, higher education, UGC and Libraries. Second chapter talks about funds where as in the third chapter infrastructure development is discussed. Chapter four gives a overview of UGC assistance for collection development under various schemes and chapter five summarises the quality improvement initiatives of the Central Government. It is followed by a bibliography of cited documents, and annexures.

The study will invite debate to know whether the facilities with university libraries are compatable to the needs of Academic world. The initiatives like INFLIBNET centre will revolutionise the future university library services. At the same time it will suggest as to what type of reorientation will suit Indian resources and manpower. The attempt is the result of professional interest of a Library and Information Scientist who has a continuous association of about 20 years with the academic and research library system.

I am thankful to the professional colleagues who inspired me all the time to record my experiences on the subject. Special thanks are due to the UGC authorities and academicians with whom I talked on the various aspects and thus benefited to produce thoughts in present form. I must mention thanks to my wife for her inspirations and thoughtful suggestions. Her constant help encouraged me to complete the work.

Thanks are also due to Concept Publishing Company who very kindly agreed to publish this work.

O.P. GUPTA

CONTENTS

LIST OF TABLES

LIST OF ANNEXURES

ABBREVIATIONS USED

AEP	Adult Education Programme
ASC	Academic Staff College
AVRC	Audiovisual Research Centres
CALIBNET	Calcutta Libraries Network
CAS	Centres of Advance Study
CDC	Curriculum Development Centre
COHSSIP	Committee on Humanities and Social Science Improvement Programme
COSIST	Committee for Strengthening Infrastructure in Science and Technology
DELNET	Delhi Libraries Network
DRS	Department of Research Support
EMRS	Educational Media Research Centre
INFLIBNET	Information and Library Network
MHRD	Ministry of Human Resource Development
NBT	National Book Trust
NEP	National Education Policy
NLM	National Literacy Mission
NPLIS	National Policy on Library and Information Science
OGL	Open General Licence
RC	Review Committee
RCLS	Review Committee on Library Science
RCSWE	Review Committee on Social Works Education
RCUGC	Review Committee on University Grants Commission
RLC	Regional Library Centre
SC/ST	Scheduled Castes/Scheduled Tribes
UGC	University Grants Commission
UNESCO	United Nations Educational Scientific and Cultural Organisation
WCCU	Working Committee on Central Universities

1

INTRODUCTION

In the process of Scientific and Technological development in last few decades, man has joined planet-to-planet race. All the countries of the world are making efforts to know the secrete of solar system. New devices are being invented to knew the hidden truth of the nature. The Camera's are working round the clock and sending photographs which are being interpreted by the scholars of all the continents. The results are being co-ordinated through advanced communication means for those who require these, are also being stored in various print and non-print forms for posterity. Such enormous flow of information records has much concern with future development programmes of the developing countries like India.

India has a very significant place among the countries of the world. It has long traditional culture and art, a land area of 23,87,263 sq. km., ever increasing population 138,760,417 (1991 Census), literacy rate 36.23, a number of castes, sub-castes and languages, etc. Inspite of all these diversities it has belief in 'Basudhaiv Kutumbakam'. Due to this strong cultural feeling of all the different sectors, people who belong to various religions, castes, colours and with other variations fought for freedom under one National Flag *Tiranga Jhanda*. For maintaining peace, unity and integrity one has to know the feelings of each other. This is one of the reasons probably, education has attracted special attention in all the times.

Education

Especially after Independence priority has been accorded to the programmes of social co-operation to remove social disparities. Illiteracy has been a great hurdle in implementing the development programmes. The system of National Education is being revised to make it relevant to the national needs, keeping in view that nothing is more important than the education. A sound national consciousness and seriousness is needed to achieve total literacy. Soon after the Second World War and Indian Independence several programmes of national reconstruction were initiated. Some of these programmes were included even in the planned development of the country.

Following five fold programme was proposed to remodle traditional education to achieve total literacy.

(i) Universal compulsory basic education for all children of school age,
(ii) Social education for our adult illiterates,
(iii) Measures for improvement in the quality and expansion of facilities for secondary and higher education,
(iv) Technical and Scientific education on a scale edequate to the nation's needs, and
(v) Measures for the enrichment of the cultural life of the community for, encouraging the arts and providing facilities for recreation and other amenities.

Even on the world scenario of Education one quarter of the world population is not able to read and write. The percentage of such persons is increasing continuously. Massive efforts therefore have been made by the world organisations to eradicate illiteracy. Since India has high percentage of illiteracy and disparities in various sectors, the immediate and appropriate attention is required. To solve the problem, all available channels of information communication should be utilised. Only after then the basic needs of the modern developing social trends can be fulfilled. To achieve goals, modernisation of library services seems an appropriate approach.

The efforts are essential to explore potentialities of all segments of the society. Due to this reason Government has launched National Literacy Mission (NLM). The Universities have also been asked to have Adult Education Programme (AEP) to achieve the goals of national reconstruction. According to UNESCO survey, one third of Indian Community even after forty years of independence is struggling with poverty for survival and which may not think of education. It is therefore, important for Indian Government and literate masses to provide education to illiterates to make them self sufficient to get food and shelter which are their primary needs. If poverty has to be eradicated or social justice has to be given to common masses then national effective educational programme has to be launched. The programmes should create environment of awareness about education and culture among masses, especially in rural, Scheduled Castes, Scheduled Tribes and backward classes of the Indian Society.

The present pattern of Indian education is more or less the same as it was initiated by the Britishers to produce manpower of their choice. If we are really prepared to change and to give fundamental right of education to all citizens for national development than thought has be given to 'knowledge explosion' and 'reading needs' of the modern society.

In ancient India the aim of education was realisation of ideals involved in *Purushartha*. As a result education came nearer to human life. It was to guide life in the direction of spiritual perfection and the sole aim became the fulfilment of life ideals i.e. *Satyam*, *Shivam* and *Sundaram*.

As we all know "Education is a key factor for future growth and development. It is a development of body, mind and spirit of each individual with his specific nature. The relation of the different studies of the growth of individual, the nature of human freedom and the need for special changes, education is the guidance to the realisation of the potentialities of each individual in the face of actual world of man and thing". Thus education has global importance during all the ages. It is a force to social advancement and modernisation.

The great revolutionary force of Indian freedom, Mahatma Gandhiji was of the view that education should guide for self support in life. Thus in Indian context, "Education is initiation in to the life of the spirit, training of human soul in the spirit of truth and the practice of virtue". It is important for survival and progress. It eradicates social complexes and prejudices to diverse cultural and social systems of the people living in various segments of the society. It brings citizens together to achieve human values for national reconstruction, all round development and also to inculcate progressive attitude to meet needs of Socio-cultural challenges of the age. It makes one conscious about the surrounding in which one lives and also about responsibilities to be shared by him. It promotes understanding of co-existance and knowledge of fundamental human rights. Thus importance of education is well accepted by the mankind of the world. Present age faster developments in the world, no society can live in isolation. The basic issue of survival has also compelled the spirit of togetherness and awareness.

Indian Constitution has a strong commitment to develop creative talent of man and women, and initiative to encourage for acquisition and dissemination of knowledge. Due to this country has made a considerable progress in last four decade in terms of increase in enrolment growth, increase in various type of Institutions and involumes of involvement and diversification of education programmes. As a result of which scholars are being produced comparable with other best Educational Institutions of the world.

Education is an integral part of the country's development process and always has been accorded high priority. Continuous efforts during the last 43 years have resulted four fold increase in the total number of literates. Universities went up to more than ten times. With quantitative expansion of educational facilities, there is now a greater emphasis on qualitative improvements. Before 1976, education was exclusively the responsibility of States, the Central Government was only concerned with certain areas like co-ordination and determination of Standards in technical and higher education etc. In 1976 through a Constitutional amendment, education became the joint responsibility of the Central and State Governments.

Thus the education in India by an large remain the subject of states concern and as a result of which and local language variations the standards in particular in higher education are different in different zones of the country. For total progress the leaders of the society and prominent educationist advised to have a central apex body to co-ordinate and suggest common guidelines to all the institutions even supervised by state or a private concerns. The idea was debated widely and finally in 1956 the University Grants Commission (UGC) was established to maintain the Standard of Higher Education in India. Further more the existing educational system which was shaped by the non-nationals with non-national interests, was remoduled with the view that higher education has to play more crucial role in modernisation and nation-building, steps were initiated for the advancement of frontiers of knowledge and research. Remodelling first step was setting up of Radhakrishnan Commission (1948-49), which recommended framing of national policies and the maintenance of standard of efficiency, liaison between universities should be the concern of the Central Government. Since than to discharge the responsibilities of Central Government and to co-ordinate facilities of university education a national central body is in operation. Maintaining standards of education is very crucial in particular when the subject is of state concern and major part of expenditure is borne by the state agencies. Inspite of variations four decade efforts of the UGC has revolutionised the entire higher education.

Even after four decade of independence the increasing number of illiterates, falling down standard of education and all round growth has invited attention to think on the issue. The educated and rich masses are putting them separate by keeping Government responsible for the cause. Recently March 1991, the subject was debated to allocate funds and Central Advisory Board on Education (CABE) which is a highest national advisory body consisting several Union Minister, State Minister of Education, Eminent Educationists and officials in its meeting held on 8-9 March, 1991 has welcomed the suggestion of raising the allocation on education to six per cent to the national income. The Board was of the view that significant increase in allocation by Central and State Governments will increase possibility of restructuring education to improve educational environment.

The University Grants Commission

To achieve the standards of Higher Education the University Grants Commission since its inception (1956) has been functioning as an autonomous statutory organisation. The UGC is appointed by the Government under an act of the parliament even then it has no direct interference in day to day working of university system. It has much wider functions than what it's name indicates. It co-ordinates and promotes university education for the determination and maintenance of standard of teaching, examination and research in universities. It has authority to enquire into financial needs of a university and to make appropriate grants to the universities. 1972 amended UGC Act has provisions 'No grant shall be given by Central Government, the Commission or any other organisation receiving any funds from the Central Government to a University which is established after the commencement of the UGC (Amendment) Act, 1972, declared such university to be fit for receiving grants, it offers advises on the establishment of new universities and matters relates with requirements of the various universities, the commission (UGC) has, followed the policy of taking the advise from people with an intimate knowledge of the problem of higher education.

UGC Act was further amended in September, 1984 to enlarge the functions of UGC for providing common facilities, services and programmes for a group of Universities or for the Universities in general. Provisions has been made to empower the UGC to determine the scales of fees charged by college to deny grants and to derecognise the college, which violates the provisions laid down in the subject by the UGC act. The UGC does exercise to allocate funds in the beginning of every plan to provide maintenance grant to the Central Universities, and development grants and other especial grants to State and Central Universities. Deemed to be universities and colleges.

The UGC to democratise the working formulates in various type of committees, etc. The power and function in detail as on Annexure 1.1 are being exercised by the UGC to maintain standards of Higher Education in the country. In recent efforts revision of pay scales of teachers, guidelines for performance appraisal, code of professional ethics, establishment of Academic Staff college for in service training and INFLIBNET programmes are important initiatives.

The Universities has been first established in India more than 2000 years ago; Two of them were 'Nalanda' and 'Taxila'. These were specialised in religious knowledge. It shows that India has a very rich educational heritage and culture. As a result of which since olden days scholars from abroad have been attracted. The present age scholars are busy in reviewing the traditional noble services. Every effort of review, suggested measures to promote quantitative as well as qualitative improvements in university education is welcomed. The Universities which took shape as state activity, the Centre through the UGC gives guidance to limit activities within identified area to keep up these relevant to the National and International needs.

Higher Education in India

With all these above efforts, the expansion of higher education in the country is not in proportion to the job opportunities. The system has inherit defects, especially most of the curriculas are out dated and irrelevant to the socio-economic needs of the society. The gradation system has local variations and similar other regional constraints of language, sources and social and political problems has effected higher education to a great extend.

This is the reason in past years many commissions and committees have been appointed, conferences, seminars and workshops were conducted, survey and case studies were made to find out solutions for improving higher education in India. The problem is widely debated and large number of articles books have been appeared in various

Indian and foreign journals which are collected by the libraries to facilities further studies and research.

The development of university libraries in the country have been parallel to the development of institutions of higher education. Therefore, it would be helpful to know the higher education or university education scenario for knowing the library system of the universities and colleges.

With UGC efforts, the population of higher education in free India has gone in many folds. It has largest educational system in the world. Universities has increased to 144 with 10 Institute of higher learning and about 25 Deemed universities. The number of affiliated colleges has gone up to 6,912. The present enrolment exceeds 5 millions. In particular higher education expansion in Engineering and Technology, Agriculture, Medicine and Allied professional areas, is very high. But growth is haphazard and unplanned. The higher education, in modern Scientific and Technological world has most significant place in the process of progress. Economic and social development, welfare and security are closely dependent on the extent and quality of higher education. Country needs unique higher education system to meet the challenges of time.

The aims and objectives of higher education have been changed after independence. Tremendous expansion to achieve political goals have been accepted by almost all the States. The Universities and Colleges were opened without taking the consent of Central Government, half of the strength of the colleges is not even today on the financial assistance list of the UGC. Even colleges like Engineering and Medical were opened without adequate facilities. Towards the close of the year 1977-78 the commission (UGC) developed a document 'Policy frame' for the development of higher education in India for next 10 to 15 years. The policy frame outlines main achievements and failures with suggestions to make education more flexible and dynamic.

"Higher education provides people with an opportunity to comprehend significant social, economic, cultural, moral and spiritual issues facing humanity today. It contributes to national development through dissemination of specialised knowledge and skills. It is therefore, crucial task of national building. Thus 'consolidation and quality improvement continued to be principal features of developments in the area of higher education."

The doyen of educational plans, Professor Dr. D.S. Kothari while discussing "Education and Values" has emphasised that adequate in quality and scale, is to the most powerful instrument for national development, welfare and society, he further adds the single most important characteristic of our times is that for the first time in men's history the world has become knowledge based, imparting to education a role and significance as never before in history. He is of the view that the electronic revolution which has let to the presence of automation, artificial intelligence, personal computers in every day use will likely be an integral component in education and is certain to have a profound impact, perhaps even greater than that of the invention of the printing press five centuries age.

With modernisation UGC is of the view that "Teaching in the class room should not be confined to lectures alone. More and more emphasis should be given to make use of modern teaching aids such as models, audio-visual aids, computers and various other electronic gadgets. The excitement of learning through computer simulation has opened up a new horizon in teaching process. Learning should not be passive but positively participative".

Review Committee and UGC programmes—Report (1981) accepted that the university system has important responsibilities to the society as a whole as well as to the educational system itself. The significance of the traditional functions, of acquisition, preservation, dissemination and extension of the frontiers of knowledge, the balanced education of individuals, and the training of high level personnel for all works of life is obvious. But a modern university, especially in a developing country like ours, has to undertake several other functions as well. It must, for instance.

— inculcate and promote basic human values and the capacity to choose between alternate value systems;
— preserve and foster our great cultural traditions and blend them with essential elements from other cultures and peoples;
— promote a rational outlook and scientific temper;
— enrich the Indian languages and promote their use as important means of communication, national development and unity;
— promote the development of the total personality of the students and inculcate in them a commitment to society through involvement in national service programme;
— act as an objective critic of society and assist in the formulation of national objectives and programme for their realization;

— promote commitment to the pursuit of excellence;
— promote the development of science and technology and of an indigenous capability to apply it effectively with special emphasis on national problems; and
— contribute to the improvement of the entire educational system so as to serve the community".

"The universities are seats of higher learning to which admission is only possible after obtaining high school leaving certificates. The objectives of each university have been set out in the various enactments governing each university". There are the Central Universities governed by central acts, state universities governed by state enactments, number of affiliated colleges and deemed universities etc. governed by their acts. Thus the universities are centre place for disseminating the advanced knowledge and works to feed a large community of students, scientists and social scientists etc. Therefore, Pt. Nehru while delivering a convocation address in 1947 said "If the universities discharge their duties adequately, than it is well with the nation and the people".

In this long journey the universities having been accepted as instruments of social change. Now through their new programmes of teaching, research and extension with the involvement of students and teachers to provide leadership to the community at large and the under-privileged community in particular. Through these new concepts of non-traditional educational system and thereby ensures the process of life long-educational opportunities for the different sectors of the community, whether urban or rural, thereby involving themselves in the total upliftment of the society which only can ensure national goals and aspirations towards the growth of a self reliant society and making it possible for the fulfilment of the dream of our late Prime Minister Pandit Jawaharlal Nehru of building a free, modern and united India.

The UGC in practice of reviewing various programmes, which are being implemented by it and the impact that these have made on the fulfilment of statutory responsibilities of it namely, determination and maintenance of standards of teaching, examinations and research in Universities. The review work is performed by a team of persons with an intimate knowledge and experience of functioning of University system in India. One such review work was carried out by a UGC Review Committee (1977) with assistance of various sub-committees. The committee visited selected Universities and Colleges to make the assessment of different stages of development, with particular reference to co-ordination and determination of standards of higher education and made recommendations conducive to more effective discharge of the responsibilities. The Committees which worked under the chairmanship of Shri V.S. Jha reviewed critically the working and various schemes in three following phases:

Phase I	August 1956 to 1961 January
Phase II	March 1961 to 1973 January
Phase III	January 1973 to 1975 March.

Second effort in this direction was formulation of a UGC Reviews Committee (1981) under the Chairmanship of Shri Satish Chandra the then Chairman, UGC. Separate committee to review the working of central universities and various schemes and similar other efforts are being made as and when are deemed necessary.

Central Universities

Working Committee on Central Universities (WCCU). (1984) recommended the objective for the central universities. The Universities as Institutions of National importance will endeavour to serve the purpose of human resource development and national advancement by providing a wide variety of educational programmes to suite the needs and aptitudes of the scholars with due regard to the manpower needs of the country. Therefore, the central universities role and responsibilities are clear, it is to function effectively and vigorously on an all India basis, to build up a corporate intellectual life in the country and to strengthen national integration. Broadly speaking, the Central Universities should provide courses which need facilities interms of staff and equipment ordinarily beyond the reach of State Universities or for which the demand would be too small. It also function to contribute towards removal of imbalance from the academic life of our country, and take suitable action to help deserving students from educationally backward areas. With this National Character central universities have been established by acts of Parliament and funds are provided by Central Government through UGC. At present following central universities are recognised in the various parts of the country.

(i) Delhi University, Delhi
(ii) Aligarh Muslim University, Aligarh
(iii) Banaras Hindu University, Varanasi
(iv) Jawaharlal Nehru University, New Delhi
(v) Hyderabad University, Hyderabad
(vi) Vishwa Bharti University, Shanti Niketan
(vii) Indira Gandhi National Open University, New Delhi
(viii) North Eastern Hill University, Shillong
(ix) Pondicherry University, Pondicherry
(x) Jamia Millia Islamia University, New Delhi.

The Universities are working as centre of higher education, teaching, research and service centre of the community. These are marching towards the objectives suggested by Pt. Jawahar Lal Nehru "A University stands for humanism, for tolerance, for reason, for the adventure of ideas and for the search of truth. It stands for the onward march of the human race towards ever higher objectives". To achieve these objectives on the university campus, in the libraries a corporate complex, teachers and students are jointly engaged in the pursuit of knowledge and in the search of truth. It has, therefore, been realised that education as a means of national development at all levels–economic, political and social, and in the development plans, universities should translate this realisation in to reality through appropriate planning of their educational programme", as well as library service development programmes.

Maulana Azad a great patriot expressed, it was Universities which has made "Solid contribution to the achievement of Indian independence by awakening a new political consciousness among large number of their alumni", therefore, steps are being taken to achieve qualitative as well as quantitative expansion of university and college education. Efforts are still continuing to promote Adult Education, Distance Education, Media Education and Women Education etc. Facilities are created for Backward Classes, Scheduled Caste and Scheduled Tribes etc. The ideas behind is that knowledge and skills will eradicate all type of problems of the individuals as well as the Society. The educational development will mean total progress of the present age Society without any reservation of Caste, Cread and Sex etc. "If we claim to be civilised, we must develop thought for the poor and the suffering, respect for women, faith in human brotherhood regardless of race or colour, nation or religion, love or peace and freedom, adherence of cruelty and ceaseless deviation to the claims of justice". For preserving real freedom and values of democracy, justice and liberty, equality and fraternity, the quality and excellence in educational activities to be maintained, the challenges of emerging area of Science and Technology to be welcomed to provide wider opportunities for vocational education of different levels to reconstruct potential for searching solutions for problems of higher education. The UGC discussed the subject with Vice Chancellors, senior Academics of the University, representatives of the State Government and with number of subject specialists and identified thrust areas for Seventh Five Year Plan keeping in view the objectives of NEP (1986). Stress was put to the following areas along with the Consolidation and expansion of various programmes of teaching and research.

Academic Staff College;
Alternative Models of Management in Universities;
Accredilation and Assessment Council;
Autonomous University/Deptt./College;
Educational Programme in Emerging Areas;
Programmes for Minorities; SC/ST; qualifying test for eligibility of Lectures Handicaps and Women;
Redesigning of Courses;
SAP and COSIST Schemes;
State Council of Higher Education; and
Youth and Sports

Eighth Plan Priorities

The Commission to further enhance the capabilities of the Universities and Colleges as active centres of teaching and research, circulated some general guidelines to formulate proposals for development during Eighth Plan period. The Universities were given areas to prepare schemes outside the plan allocations. On receipt of the proposals and discussion with University authorities, the Commission has identified thrust areas and recommended following special centres during Eighth plan.

Weaker Sections;
Rural Development;
Disaster Studies;

Fabrication of Low Cost Equipment;
Tribal Studies;
Vocational Studies;
Office Automotion;
Energy and Environmental Studies;
North Eastern Region Studies;
National Integration;
Nepal Studies;
Re-structuring of Courses;
Santhal Studies;
Studies in National Security;
Development of City Centres;
Visual and Performing Arts;
Science in Society;
Studies in SC & ST;
Buddhist Studies;
Regional Planning and Rural Development;
Women Entrepreneurship;
Career Counselling Guidance and Coaching;
Drought and Famine;
Folklore and Folk-Culture;
Public Affairs;
National Harmony and Integration and
Himalayan Studies.

The rate of growth in the research out-put of the world has been so high that the volume of knowledge is doubling with in a short period of 10 to 15 years. Co-operation therefore, is very much necessary, to set up common library services, to pool efforts and resources for developing specialities and to under take joint programmes of research and teaching etc. The specialised knowledge developed in the University should be available to other Universities. It is also essential due to explosion in knowledge and in enrolment in universities and colleges. As India claims to have third largest country in university and college population. The development needs a radical change in organisation and in the method of teaching and examinations. The studies should be strengthened with diversified courses and various aptitudes and abilities.

New method of teaching out side the classroom have become very popular almost in all the disciplines. A good numbers of Open

Universities and University Departments are engaged in imparting Distance Education. Similarly the concept of Media Education has come up and in recent future, every University library has to create a Media cell to keep track on the lectures prepared under this programme. The change and new schemes has put special emphasis on the effective and intensive use of library collections. The UGC has regarded support for research as individual excellence as well as social concern.

Recent development in Political and Technological spheres in the country, call for a re-apprasial of the University Libraries functions, alongwith traditional services of preservation and communication of existing knowledge should work to develop in modern technological out look. This requires a re-interpretation and adaptation of our traditional values in the context of changed values. Particularly University Libraries should ensure that they are influencing or effecting to the thinking of their users. Which will produce a modern progressive academic community.

The study reveals that "With the explosion of knowledge, the methodology of teaching and the contents of education itself have gone under change. The system of higher education must, therefore, be dynamic. Even than frequent changes may not be advisable to disturb the tenor of higher education, but it does not mean that the system should be stagnant. It is obvious that the essential dynamism of higher education requires suitable changes in the existing administrative and academic machinery in the universities". The content of education are continuously oriented towards fundamental values — unity and integrity, cultural consciousness, democracy, secularism, environment and problems of population growth etc.

University education has manifold function to discharge. Pursuit of excellence in knowledge and advancement of knowledge have been the main functions of University education. This approach, however, is no longer adequate in the context of rapid national development, and social change. The function of a University to-day is not only to enable the students to attain excellence in knowledge, but also to contribute directly to national development, to furnish intellectual and moral leadership to the community at large. To-day when our nation is struggling to march towards the establishment of a modern society, bases on political and economic justice and social equality, university education can no longer remain a passive spectator. The task of creating a new social order which has assumed paramount importance to-day can not be overlooked by the university community.

Gujandra Gadkar Committee stressed that equally important, is the challenge of the expansion of knowledge. The lack of competency at the part of teacher and taught should be eradicated. The conditions in higher education be improved, in Institutions of higher learning where standards are very deplorable due to inadequate resources.

The selected Scholars should only be encouraged for further studies with incentives. Standards of University Education Report (1965) also recommended teaching aids like radio, television, machines, films, tap records and so on can be used with great advantage by Indian Universities and Colleges. Efforts should be made to develop books in regional languages. Since the recorded knowledge is the basis of further studies, therefore, a point of view of recorded knowledge should be put forward in the general curricula of the studies.

History of Knowledge Records

History of the men on the earth is the history of knowledge. Right from the beginning of the society till today there has always been a constant social pressure to find out some thing new. Thus the present day knowledge is the result of social needs, revolution and human requirement. Man is inpractices of using his mental faculties in expanding the horizons of comforts of luxuries of life. For the benefit of the posterity, acquired knowledge in the beginning was recorded or preserved on stones, clay, bone pieces, or parchment, leaves and papyrus etc. Later with the advancement of paper and printing technology the knowledge is being stored in the form of books or print form. Modernisation and continuous scientific efforts have increased new subjects, subject branches, sub-branches, interdisciplinary and socio scientific concepts. To make full use of tremendous expansion of human efforts and knowledge timely steps are needed. Otherwise with the fast developmental speed a good amount of knowledge may go waste or may not be used by the coming generations.

The conventional system of information collection has got variety and also variety in users. With the alround advancement and knowledge explosion which is taking place in every branch reason for Information records are designed in various forms. In recent past technological development has also revolutionised the library collections and services as well. The libraries of modern age are suppose to work as 'communication centres'. The pressure of keeping non book materials such as microfilms, microstrips, video-audio cassettes, computer disks, floppies etc. is increasing in all type of libraries, throughout the country. Before going to the present days University library scenario a brief note on history development of libraries will be helpful in knowing the growth of academic libraries.

History of Libraries

History of libraries is as old as men himself. Perhaps, all rich traditions in all fields: Education: Art and Culture, in olden times were preserved for future generations. Those steps resulted the social Institutions i.e. Libraries. The libraries in the beginning were recognised by their collections. Keeping of books was a status symbol. Such collections were recognised as great institutions of civilisation and culture. Libraries took birth as hobby of the individual, the collections were of their choice and interest. In their rich heritage these collections and the places where these books were stored become keeper of our heritage and culture.

The freedom of free development resulted a strong feeling that libraries should grow in all directions. These should preserve all type of documents. The feeling is still continuing in all type of libraries whether maintained by Government or by private agencies. Even the University library for a long time developed in the wims of influencing scholars or with donated collections without taking in notice of the requirements. At least the present university libraries expension is free from such practices. Though there is no national policy as well as libraries policy for systematic growth and especialised advancement. Inspite of all efforts the collections have gone multidisciplinary and so huge that a large part of these remains beyond the reach of the users.

Libraries

The library is central to the whole business of education. This may be the reason probably Prof. J.H. Shera conceives library as a human enterprise. It is live Social Institution drawing its life and birth through the services of people working as a team to achieve the common ends of dissemination of knowledge and the freedom of human mind and intellect. Every library is trinity of three units.

(i) Reading material (collection)
(ii) Reader (Users)
(iii) Place of reading (Building)

Similarly every library has following primary task to perform

(i) Acquisition
(ii) Organisation of collections
(iii) Services to disseminate knowledge.

In present era libraries are known for their services not for collections. Though these depositories are continuing traditional lending and accepting modernisation in the form of technology. In the present era information use have become a necessity of all the sections, it may be Politicians, Businessmen, Scientists or Scholars of any discipline. Library is a place where variety of activities/information designed to promote better understanding of volumes and characteristics. It is a forum of mutual trust, cooperation, goodwill, self-help, self-confidence, self-reliance and initiative. It disseminates the preserved knowledge and information among the world population irrespective of caste, creeds and sex etc. It also generats moral intellectual, spiritual and social values in the masses. As a reult of which the less and under-privileged classes comes with more encouragement for socio-economic development of the country.

The Printing Technology and Mass Media has increased the information in many folds. But simple increase of information may not be the development. The full use of increased information is very essential otherwise it will go waste and it will be a total loss to the nation. For using increased documents/information user co-ordination is needed.

Libraries for Academic Advancement

Library is a heart and soul of any academic programme. It is an asset to the Institution to which attached in particular to run research programmes, it has very significant role to play. Libraries are the institutions which equally feed to teacher and taught. Indeed in transmission of knowledge one place to another or individual to another, library services has very effective role. There has been a considerable development in the library services in free India. Credit goes to late Dr. S.R. Ranganathan to flow the current of library services all around the citizens of the country. The libraries are the informal institutions of education, which are most democratic institutions and centres for dissemination of global knowledge of all the times.

These are the keepers of our history and culture. Development of library system is an important component of the scheme of non-formal and continuing education. Constitutionally the subject 'libraries' is included in State list. Centre has jurisdiction only over libraries established by it and institutions of national importance as declared by it. There are more than 60,000 libraries in the country.

Libraries in India, on one hand preserve cultural heritage of the country, on the other hand it incorporates changes taking place time to time. It brings together to all the regions, religious beliefs, languages, life styles, etc. In this process it assimilates old and new to produce modern. In this way it shapes society. Review Committee on Library Science (RCLS) (1965) emphasised the importance of libraries at the present stage of development of our country, and said that without libraries, public education, which is essential in a democracy, cannot be promoted. We are therefore, developing a network of libraries in the country. The demand for library service has grown further with the democraticisation of the country.

"Libraries are now Universally recognised as an important social institutions for diffusion of knowledge and information. No Community, Institution or Organisation is considered complete without the support of a library and its effective services. The gradual spread of the concept of democracy, extension of education, intensification of research activity, rapid industrialisation, continuous increase in production of recorded knowledge both in print and non-print form, and advancement in information, computer and communication technologies have contributed to the growth of libraries and information centres to develop user-oriented services."

Nation is well aware that information infrastructure and modernisation of the library system are essential to aim at Scientific, Technological and Economic progress and attain eminence. It has therefore, realised that the investments in library systems and their modernisation are worth for evolving an information oriented society. It is also required to reduce the widening gap between developed and developing countries in utilisation of information and knowledge. Otherwise there will a danger of continued information dominance of the developed countries over the rest of the world. In other words, information poor countries will continue to lag behind to information rich countries.

As a result of it, the Government of India, in its various national policy and planning documents, has stressed upon the importance of information in national development and has talked for free flow of information. Document on National Policy on Library and Information Science (NPLIS) 1986' reached to the conclusion that India must have a National Policy on Library and Information System, because library and Information services are required to provide the basic inputs for planning and modernising different sectors of education, culture and economy. While setting objectives of the policy it was accepted that library and Information sources are vital for all sectors of national activity. The availability of information expeditiously and pinpointedly, supports decision-making processes at all tends. Relevant information accelerates the national development. An informed citizen is an asset to a democratic system of government and the proper utilisation of information can improve the quality of citizens. The Government of India, therefore, realises the value of coordinating and upgrading the existing library and information systems and services, initiating new programmes relevant to our national needs, taking advantage of the latest advances in Information technology. The National Policy on Library and Information has suggested following aims:

(i) To foster, promote and sustain, by all appropriate means, the organisation, availability and use of information in all sectors of national activity;

(ii) To take steps for mobilising and upgrading the existing library and information systems and services and initiating new programmes relevant to our national needs, taking advantage of the latest advances in information technology;

(iii) To encourage and initiate, with all possible speed, programmes for the training of library and information personnel, on a scale and of a calibre adequate to provide the library and information services and to recognise their work as an important component of the quality and level of such services;

(iv) To set up adequate monitoring mechanisms for ensuring a rapid development of library and information facilities and services for meeting the information needs of all sectors and levels of the national economy;

(v) To encourage individual initiative for the acquisition and dissemination of knowledge, and for the discovery of new knowledge in an atmosphere of intellectual freedom;

(vi) In general, to secure for the people of the country all the benefits that can accrue from the acquisition and application of knowledge; and

(vii) To preserve and make known the nation's cultural heritage in its multiple forms.

In the last four decades after independence much has been discussed to develop the libraries. The role of library and information centres has been recognised in every sphere of national reconstruction. Multi directional growth has increased number of libraries, books and professionals. The fact has been very well visualised by the Policy makers, Academicians, and Library Scientists and they are more library conscious then ever before. Therefore, it is the moral obligation of the librarians that they should accept the task of dissemination of the preserved knowledge and, also to put it into generation of new knowledge. The efforts will enrich knowledge and eradicate certain social constraints.

In recent developments over all educational change was very much demanded by the National Education Policy (NEP), 1986. Librarians, library information scientists has to initiate for improving the existing services for encouraging users for seeking the information documents. The present age Scientific and Technological progress is fully dependent on modernised library services. The books should become part and partial of every one's life. This inculcated habit through libraries will invite social revolution and national unity in progressive Indian Community.

Modernisation

If we talk on the progress of last two decades the country is preparing for 21st Century. The electronic revolution has brought out innovations in the field of Information Technology. Modernisation has gifted mechanised preservation and dissemination of the information. The Scientists and Academicians are thinking for online service and networking of information system. Keeping in view the advancement in technology and many folds increase in information. Government has initiated number of steps. Now the documents are given due recognition and have been taken out from the store items list of Government. The orders for dealing with the unwanted document has been issued by Ministry of Finance. Documents for formulating

National Policy for Library and Information Science (NPLIS) for providing adequate library services to the masses of the country, has developed the programmes to use large number of academic, public, special and departmental libraries for active participation of their users. The document prepared for NPLIS has laid more emphases on the following areas:

(i) Resource Sharing;
(ii) SDI/CAS Services;
(iii) Modernisation/Computer Application;
(iv) Use of Micro Processor;
(v) Network of Library and Information Science Centre;
(vi) Quality of Personal engaged in the profession;
(vii) User Education Programme; and
(viii) Quality of service to be improved.

The use of library will create understanding in users about their rights. They will also know the other's achievements. The competition will encourage them to think about themselves and about others also.

As a result of increased activity knowledge is expanding tremendously and the expansion can be treated as knowledge expansion. With slow increase we were nearer to our heritage or past but with speedy change it is not within the reach of the present generation. As implications of the explosion, present day student/user has to read more. In this way self study have become more important.

Library is a live agency to promote education. Professor Yashpal, Ex-Chairman, UGC, a leading Scientist in his forward of INFLIBNET report has stressed that "the role and growth of information and knowledge is faster than ever before and still accelerating. There are enormous number of new developments both in applications and pure thought. He, further add that the education and creative members of the society should have quick access to whatever is happening in their own country and the world over.

It is assumed that whole of the knowledge generated throughout the world is shared through the various type of publications such as Book, and Journals. If it is true than an good substance of knowledge is not reaching to the scholars of universities and colleges as the universities are not in a position to purchase each and every published document. This handicape of purchasing the new arrivals is with each and every institutions. If we want to run with the International development speed than a quick access to what is being done in the country and abroad must be established by removing all constrains of distance, language and other man made barriers.

Use of Libraries

The importance of the books/information is very much debated by the Scholars. In classroom teaching, the teacher in the fast advancing scientific period is in difficulty to provide knowledge of each and every development of the subject. It is not possible for teacher to know everything even that has to be known in the field of his specialisation. In a class lecture only a broad out line of the subject is given. To get the comprehensive knowledge one has to depend on the books which are generally available in libraries. The real learning can be performed in the libraries. It is, therefore, becomes essential for students to come closer to libraries to establish relation with the books.

Library is a heart of the university education. It is a treasure house of knowledge even then during pre-independence period university libraries were not paid much attention. The number of such library was very less. It is only after independence and establishment of the UGC and with the help of Scholars like Dr. C.D. Deshmukh, Dr. D.S. Kothari, Prof. Dr. S.R. Ranganathan and Prof. Yashpal, all round progress in the communication centres i.e libraries has been noticed.

The University libraries has important responsibility to the society as a whole as well as to the educational system itself. The significance of the traditional functions of acquisition, preservation, processing, dissemination of information for extension of frontiers of knowledge for all walks of life is obvious.

The adequate library services within such institutions were developed for raising the standard of higher education in the country. After independence high priority has been accorded to develop appropriate collections and also attention has been paid to provide necessary equipment to cope with the application of the modern technology. In pre-independence era the universities and the college for years together in the country continued without adequate building, collection and organised services. In the beginning the collections were housed in some less used area in the custody of some caretaker clerical staff. A new light spread with the expansion of research, when the honorary librarians were identified from the scholars to promote library services. Than the libraries were realised as Information

Service Centres.

The Scholars, Library Incharges made recommendations to put full time professionally trained librarians in the universities and the colleges to expand library service. Even today with all progressive steps old traditional restrictions in Institutional libraries are continued. A good number of libraries without professional librarians and without organised library services, are working almost in all the parts of the country.

The UGC in its journey of about thirty four years has set up a number of committees namely, Ranganathan Committee, (1965), Carlwhite's Survey of Delhi University recommendations of the committee on standards of Education, Review Committee of central universities, committee on pay scales — Mehrotra Committee, Workload Committee and INFLIBNET programme etc. to bring the concept that the libraries are temple of learning and professionals working in these regarded as interpreter of knowledge.

University Libraries Development

Rich heritage of the culture and civilisation has been preserved in the libraries since olden times. Especially the university libraries are educative in their nature. This task has become more important with Information Explosion. Human knowledge is increasing very fast. Therefore, to access to information pin pointedly exhaustively and expeditiously organised university library services have become essential. The UGC has propagated library consciousness in Academic Community to a long way. University library services have been mainly revolutionised on the recommendations of Dr. S.R. Ranganathan pioneer Library Scientist of the century. The library in university system occupies a significant and crucial place, because all the functions of teaching and research are served by it. To accept modern teaching techniques as well as improved self learning system the libraries has to be regarded very important. Considering the importance of libraries in higher education, the UGC is in practice of appointing various committees for studying the problems referred by the Academic Institutions as well as by professionals to improve the library services. The very first and serious attention to university and college library in free India was paid by Dr. C.D. Deshmukh. The University libraries, and professional staff working in their remains behind the scene where it works to modernise the higher education.

This may be one of the reason sometimes it looks like an ignorance of library services. Infact, good quality service had enhanced the possibilities of new areas of service. The UGC which was established to maintain standard of higher education has always stressed the importance of libraries in maintaining standards. In higher education intensive use of libraries is involved because the knowee supplements his studies with the views of those who have established parametres in the field of study. For such efforts a good library is required. Inspite of favourable recommendations of Commissions and Committees about importance of library in university system the present scenario reveals to the inadequate facilities.

Aim of Higher Education is to import especialised and advanced knowledge for alround social progress. Higher education is to build up one's to contribute to knowledge. It is an attempt to cultivate and develop excellence to change the traditional thinking. It is pre-required in modern world where progress has basis of free flow of information. Library is the main agency to discharge this activity. This is also to established that we are superior among the living creations of the nature because of our brain. For keeping brain healthy and bright use of books seems essential.

Expansion

Growth in higher education and in university libraries is well accepted which has not been co-ordinated and channelised in a purposeful direction. About two lakhs of science journals and six lakhs titles of books annually added to academic libraries. For making effective use of these huge collections Organised System of university and college library is an important need. These libraries are expanding in parallel lines. There is no close relation with University Library and College Library for any purpose, may be technical treatment of literature or policy frame etc. These are only looking for Inter Library Loan in some cases. College libraries are not fully developed. Library development is inadequate due to speedy growth in Enrolment, Staff, Researchers, and enormous increase in volumes of Information. It is also due to lack of sound national policy plan.

Present day university libraries policy will build up future library services "planning of library services, therefore, is regarded as one specific aspect of educational planning within the social and economic planning of a country, within this context library planning acquire the foundation of support that it needs, if it is to be effective." The planning, therefore, of library services implies a continuous systematised process of studying educational problems. Not only this, it also involves determining the aims of library services, setting the target for attaining those aims and preparing decision to ensure that those objectives will be fulfilled through the rational available resources.

According to the Association of Indian Universities (AIU), National Policy on University Libraries 'A University library is no longer part of an ivory tower world, it is a practical, service institutions accountable for every aspect of its performance'.

Though the library service is highly debated subject in Periodicals, Books and Seminars Symposia etc. even then no serious attempts have been made so far to access the value and relevance of the library science education imparted in the university departments or by some of the Library Associations. The standard of the library training course contents differ widely from one department to other library science department. No uniformity in the pattern of papers, admission, qualification, practical training and relevance of the course contents to the job requirement of the zone of the library school belongs, has been maintained.

The need of improving the standards of teaching and research in the department of library and information science has been realised by the UGC and a Curriculum Development Committee (CDC) has been set up to make complete review of the subject as well as to modernise the existing syllabi to make it more relevant with the Technological development of the century.

For democratic common approach and for common purpose co-ordinated development (Networking) of library and information centres is an urgent need of the nation. It will bring quality in services. Libraries will be able to work as centres for self directed learning which in turns will be full use of human resources. The library services should be expanded to the reach of every one in every condition. It should not be restricted in any case.

Modernisation has accepted application of technology to cope with the faster growth. At present country people has general feeling that technology will minimise the job opportunities and this fear of pushing youth towards unemployment prevent them to accept the new light coming from the Scientific and Technical development of the world. Where the modernisation will generate potential and creative thinking for understanding International socio-cultural linkages.

To get the proper return of resources the UGC has to get cooperation of the universities in promotion and understanding of the academic and technical functions of a modern library staff. Libraries has come a longway in meeting the challenges of modern information science and Information technology for fastering by implementing computer to develop a Information culture in Indian Academic population.

Recommendations of Commissions and Committees for the Growth of University Libraries

The library facilities before independence in most of colleges and universities were very poor. The conditions were poor in terms of buildings, collections and professional staff. As a result these were less used. Where the libraries are the keeper of our history and culture. For Academic/University Libraries Education Commission (1948-49) made observation that the library is the heart of all the university's work directly. For the humanistic research the library is the both library and laboratory in one and therefore, a first class library is essential in a university.

Similarly Kothari Commission (1964-66) paid attention to the development of University and Colleges Libraries. It recommended that:

(i) "The heads of departments and library staff should co-operate fully in drawing up an integrated plan of library development, from a long range point of view. Such a plan should take into consideration a number of factors such as anticipated increase in enrolment, the facultywise distribution of students, new subjects and fields of specialization, special research projects, and so on.

(ii) No new university college or department should be set up without taking into account its library needs in terms of staff, books, journals, space etc. Because nothing could be more damaging to a growing department than to neglect its library or to give it a low priority. On the contrary the library should be an important centre of attraction on the college or university campus. Library therefore, should

— provide resources necessary for research in the fields of special interest to the university,
— aid the university teachers in keeping abreast of development in their field,
— provide library facilities and services necessary for the success of ill formal programmes of instruction,
— open the door to widen world of books that lie beyond the boarders of one's field of specialisation, and
— to loaning books, students and scholars together under conditions which encourage reading for pleasure, self discovery, personal growth and the sharpening of intellectual curiosity.

To achieve the goals of higher education and efficiency, the working of university libraries has been reviewed at various stages by the UGC. The first effort in this regard was the 'Development of University and College Libraries, (1965)' under the Chairmanship of Dr. S.R. Ranganathan, Library Scientist of the age. The Committee reviewed the library services in their totality and made recommendations for UGC grants, library funds, book selection and book purchase, promotion of reading habit, weedingout the loss of books, documentation, departmental collection, library staff, Deptts. of Library Sciences and library buildings, fittings and furniture etc. and for systematic development of university and college libraries in the country.

Review Committee on University Grants Commission (RCUGC) (1977) was also library conscious and expressed "use of a library is itself a technique and unless students are trained to use libraries they may not derive any benefit, the matter needs attention, the main emphasis should be put to improvement of library facilities.

Review Committee on University Grants Commission (RCUGC) (1981) was also of the view universities should draw up integrated plans of library development from a long range point of view. An essential thing about the development plan of a university library is to consider it from the academic rather than the financial point of view. Even more important is the proper use of books by students and teachers. Lectures should be supplemented by tutorial instructions and therefore, the student should turn to the library to find relevant materials for themselves, with the help of reference librarians. More working hours and working days, easy accessibility to books, designing of library as a centre of community education and cultural activities, multiple copies of text books which may be loaned to needy students, a better display of new reading materials, organisation of book clubs, exhibition, paintings, tape-records of classical music, separate rooms for periodicals, reference books and research work, are some of the measures that would help in raising the standard of library service and utilisation of available resources. The reading habit both on the part of teacher and students is low in most of the universities, and attention should be paid to improve in every possible way.

Review of Social Works Education in India (RSWEI) Report (1981) also analysed the scenario of libraries. It noticed that the position with regard to libraries was very unsatisfactory. Even where libraries are shared with other departments of a college or university. It is necessary for the department to have its own specialised collections. Especially, as books are very expansive and most of the student cannot afford them. With an ever increasing enrolment in universities and college and demands for books and journals has been constantly growing. Unlike in the past university libraries have now to cater to the diversified needs of undergraduates, postgraduates, and research scholars.

The academic library system including the university and college libraries forms sector for research. The pressing need here is to explore the needs for and study the problems arising from making teaching library centred. The departments of Library Science in the collaboration with other organisation should pursued research to solve the problems faced by the profession.

University and college library should observe the following programmes.

1. Collection of information:
   Acquisition of Book and Journals,
   Exchange of Publication,
   Nonprint material,
   Organisation of lecture,

2. Dissemination of Information;
   Equipped and well trained staff,
   Reference service,
   user education,
   well conversant with Modern Services,
   Technological use; Computer CD-ROM etc.

Here it will be pertinent to mention that in present age only one institution i.e. library in all changes circumstances throughout the glob is rendering service in most democratic manner. The libraries have been shelter all time and good guide in all ups and downs of the lifes of the countries and individuals. These are working as the communication or dissemination centres of the collected knowledge and guide of education to all mankind for global development. It is, therefore, becomes essential that thought should be given to 'knowledge explosion' and 'reading needs' of the modern society.

Indian Govt. has put stress on the role of education for human resource development vide its National Education Policy (NEP) document, 1986. For National development or for bringing over all socio-economic development in the country programme of education for all has been launched and it will make every one aware of fast going development of every sphere of life. The awareness required for the dignity of men and for progress and prosperity of the nation as well. Knowledge has very close link with the progress. A progress without free flow of information cannot be imagin. The libraries are the place where the knowledge of information is acquired preserved and disseminated expeditiously and pin pointedly. To achieve the goals of library services efforts have been made to improve collections, preservation facilities as well as services approaches. The modern approach towards libraries is to recognise these as information centres instead of store houses of books.

History development of university libraries reveals that even today, we have not been able to develop a sound universities library system. We are not using resources effectively even though the libraries are the backbone of the university education system. New Technological development has opened a new era for library house jobs and services. Almost all the advanced countries has started on line date access. Million of Records are kept on hundreds of Data-base. The automated information services has brought over all revolution in the library services.

In India, use of computer in libraries is very slow. Although a number of special libraries or departmental libraries and Information centres have taken lead in using computers. But the development in university and college libraries yet to take place. Expectations are that eighth plan will create environment to implement the advanced technologies.

Review Committee on central universities; University of

Hyderabad Report (1987) recorded a few suggestions towards the future development of the library. There is first of all a clear need for providing modern facilities such as micro-film reader, microfische reader, enlarger and printer. Need for computer based information retrieval and library management is also indicated. Provisions of micro-computer for unit operations such as circulation, acquisitions, serial control, maintenance of data for library, problem solving and decision making is important. There should also be a provision for a versatile main frame computer particularly for creating bibliographic data base for documents stored in the library. Such computer retrievals should have at least 50 terminals spread over the departments in the campus.

Changes occurring in the media for storage from floppy discs to optical storage devices and the modern methods of information handling techniques, however, will call for continuous education of the library personnel. This may be arranged by sending the library personnel to short-term courses conducted by institutions such as the Documentation Research and Training Centre, Bangalore, the Indian Scientific Documentation Centre, New Delhi, National Information Centre, New Delhi, the UGC Workshops at different Regional Centres may also be tapped for this purpose.

Eighth Plan Provision for Library Facilities

In Eighth plan guidelines under the broad directions for development schemes the commission has laid emphasis on the upgradation of library facilities and services. Libraries should be transformed into information centres and steps be taken to link the library with various departments through modern communication technology. Library services be strengthened to extent its access with a view to make it whole day Institution working with modern facilities including computer, search and documentation services.

While suggesting Universities about the criteria of develop or developing department the UGC has also taken library facilities as an important variable and the collection strength of books, journals and back volumes of journals have been given due consideration. It has suggested a formula for developing points on following pattern to select the departments for special assistance.

Books	*Point*
Over 2,000 different titles of books	2
Less than 2000 but with in 1000	1
Below 1000	0

Journals	*Point*
At least subscribing for 20 journals and have back volumes for past 20 years	2
At least subscribing for 10 journals and have back volumes for past 10 years	1

In general approaches it has also emphasised the need 'to further enhance the capabilities of the universities as active centres of teaching and research.' To give priority to strengthen existing post graduate departments library service facility should be given priority. Every efforts should be made to ensure optimal use of these services.

Mass literacy movement is the main thought for Eighth Plan to promote Adult Education, the UGC has given directives to develop proposals to upgrade library facilities for making the programme a great success.

Especially the researchers need a more intensive type of service. For which the librarian has to work constantly to provide new useful materials to the researchers for their concentrated research work. A library is a service institution. All efforts should be made to bring reader near to the book. The librarian of this age have become a Communication Officer instead of custodian of books and Journals as he was in this beginning. The beginning of it has been made by the Ministry of Finance by changing the designation of librarian as Library and Information Officer in various Government Departments.

The objective of the Eighth Plan efforts will be development of scientific temperament and awareness on the impact of science in society. Thus the important area of study may include.

Environmental Education,
Legal Literacy,
National Integration,
Population Education, and
Planning forums etc.

Keeping in view the requirements of the major thrust areas during

Eighth plan period for library development will be of greater use of new teaching methods such as audio-visual systems, interacting learning through computer etc., operation of non-book forms of knowledge records such as thousands of data base created by the university sector as well as other agencies.

University Library Scenario

As per the records of the study brought out by a INFLIBNET project 1988, there are 179 university level institutions and over 5,500 colleges with over 2,25,000 faculty staff and 40 lakhs students, of which about 40,000 are research scholars and over 3,50,000 are post graduate students. The number is increasing every year. Some universities are old and were established in the later half of last century, while a few have been founded even eighties. The teaching and research in universities are centred around their libraries. The university libraries are not uniform in their level of development. There are a few constituent, government and private affiliated colleges functioning under the jurisdiction of universities. Though the university library expected to help the college libraries in their development and to establish linkages with them, these does not, exist at present, and thus there is no inter-connection.

College Education

In the expansion and development of Indian Higher Education, the role of colleges is well known. About 85 per cent of the students receiving higher education in the colleges. The number of college has reached to 10,000 and students in lakhs. The UGC is taking steps since beginning to improve the facilities in the colleges which fulfils its guidelines. Reason for it may be the quality of university education in India will largely depend on the standards maintained by colleges and unless it is made possible for them to improve their staff, equipment, libraries, laboratory and other facilities, no real improvement of University Education will be possible. Review Committee on Social Works Education (RCSWE) (1981) of UGC also has recommended that the library is a vital aspect of an Educational Institution. It has recommended that a new college must start with a minimum of 1,500 volume in the library. This is necessary in the interest of meaningful studies at the post graduate level and for research work. It must start with 2,000 books if it has more than one programme e.g. bachelor's and master's. In addition to, the library must subscribe to at least 20 journals in the beginning of its establishment and gradually build up the number of such journals. The stock of books should be built up, within the first few years to 10,000 in respective discipline. In Eighth plan development proposals guidelines for Colleges, UGC has stressed mainly on four aims.

(a) Improvement of standards and quality of education,
(b) Removal of disparities and regional imbalances in higher educational facilities,
(c) Restructuring and diversification of courses, and
(d) Granting of autonomous status to deserbing Colleges.

The UGC will provide assistance to eligible Colleges to meet their basic needs of books and Journals including strengthening of Book Banks and Technical Staff etc. Thought has been given to eradicate disparities and regional imbalances to develop the colleges falling in backward, rural and border areas. While preparing development proposal the College may include proposals for –

(a) Books and Journals including setting up of Book Banks and/or strengthening the existing Book Banks with a view to augmenting the facilities and improving reading habits among the students;
(b) Equipment needed for improving the standards,
(c) Additional technical staff,
(d) Data collection
(e) Construction and extension of various type of Libraries.

The Pattern of Assistance decided for various items is as under:

Item	*UGC Share*
Books and Journals including Book Banks	100%
Audio-Visual equipment	100%
Library Buildings	100%

The College are expected to utilise 20 per cent of the total ceiling for books/Journals, 20 per cent of the total ceiling for equipment 40 per cent for building projects etc. In addition to general development the

UGC has a number of special programmes for improving the quality of college education.

Development Grants to Constituent Colleges

To the constituent Colleges of Delhi University as per guidelines for purchase of library Books and Journals and library contingencies an expenditure equivalent to Rs. 10 per student on roll subject to a maximum of Rs. 10,000 in addition to the actual fees collected for library and reading room, by a college is treated as approved expenditure, for purpose of payment of the annual maintenance grant. In addition to this the expenditure that may be recommended by the committee appointed by Delhi University for the colleges which are permitted to start functioning newly or to start in additional subjects and approved by the UGC are treated as approved expenditure for the purpose of payment of grant on 50 : 50 basis. As a policy grant not exceeding Rs. 50,000 will be paid to college for starting B.Sc. (Pass) classes in Group A subject to actual expenditure of the above amount.

For maintenance grant to constituent colleges for library Books, Journals, Magazines, Newspapers and contingent expenditure (Building-library accessories) cataloguing, Cabinets, Racks for Stack and Counter and for Library Books was provided as on Table 22.

The Indian Higher Education System includes all discipline like Agricultural, Technological, Medical, Institutes of Management and various general type, university and colleges established by either Central Government or by State Government or by any type of private body may have all the subject or some selected subjects. The libraries, therefore, suppose to have collections in all disciplines and also on allied areas of study.

To achieve the standards of higher education and also to improve quality, adequate library services are very much essential. To develop standard services two type of co-ordination is needed. One within the University library system and second among the libraries of the District Region, Country, Continent and so on.

During the last four decades there has been a unplanned growth of libraries which has badly effected the services. The number of enrolments and library resources has not been taken in consideration while preparing development proposals. The effect of media and increasing research output, new techniques of information production and variety in use have also not duly taken care, as a result the libraries are developing in haphazard manner and not in intensive use.

There is such a variety of university and college libraries that it would be difficult to put them in one Uniform policy for development. Previous efforts and university libraries growth reveals that there is a considerable advantage in adopting a certain degree of variability, which is essential for innovation-cum-development. For standardisation rigid policy should not be followed. To provide effective library services a continuous and systematic, approach to know the needs of education system as well as library service centres has to be evolved. Keeping in view the expansion of Distance Education. Adult Education, Woman Education, Rural Education and Population Education high priority be accorded to establish Study Centres in the allied areas.

To provide proper education in university/college to make students familiar with the Cultural, Political, Social and Economic developments, proper information dissemination will be a immediate need, which will be achieved by a sound information network. Library services should be improved qualitatively as well as quantitatively to meet the specialised need of the modern academic society. The services has close concern with the infrastructure, collections and professional skill available in the libraries. In subsequent chapters these aspects will be analysed to bring out the complete picture of present conditions.

2

FUNDS/RESOURCE DEVELOPMENT

After independence, Higher Education System in India has got multiple responsibilities to satisfy increasing qualitative and quantitative demands. This is because, higher education even has reached to the doors of weaker sections of the Society. National Education Policy (1986) demanded rural education. And in latest efforts Ramamurthy Review Committee is also suggesting plan to prompote education for rural upliftment. The UGC is co-ordinating the demands and available resources to maintain minimum standards of Indian higher education system. If we see the higher education scenario of the country over the last four decades the growth in 1988-89 was 144 Universities, 25 Institutions deemed to be Universities, 6,912 UGC funded colleges and about 39,47,922 students enrolled in University System.

Section 10 para 01 of the UGC Annual Report puts emphasis that in all development programmes library books and journals and well equipped services have a direct or indirect bearing on the well-being of the students and in promotion of congenial environment and conditions for pursuing academic programmes, to promote the work of teaching and active research and to achieve the goals of higher learning.

The improved services can be planned only when adequate funds are available to implement innovations. Funds are not only required to welcome new additions but also maintain to traditional developments. The need of funds in Indian environment are alarming due to various reasons of fast developments. In particular expansion of education conscious society and technological revolution effects at large.

Funds

Funds has key position in the implementation of the policies. Similarly the growth of libraries and library services has very close relation with the availability of funds. These are required to create basic infrastructure and to build up collections as well as to provide quality of Service. Sometimes Special Assistance is needed to meet the emerging requirement or to implement latest researches and technologies taking place to revolutionise the present situations. If we see the library progress of last few decades the forms of knowledge records have been transferred from book to electronic forms like films, disks, floppies, cassettes etc. The various house jobs of the libraries even in India are being performed by computer to achieve more efficiency and accuracy. All these technological development efforts needs regular and adequate funding to keep services compatable to National or International level. Increasing cost of documents, equipment and expenditure of salaries has made funds most important factor in organisation of modern university library services. The managers of libraries are always busy in debates to search the solution of the problem.

Sources

The University libraries are getting their funds either from Central Government, State Government, students or from some voluntary contributions of Individuals or Organisations. All voluntary efforts may contribute for a particular scheme or for a particular time and amount may vary. These supporting agencies may withdraw their support at any time. Which results fluctuation in funds collection. Where the requirements will compell to generate a minimum amount on a particular point of time to meet regular expenditures. The regular funds are also required to meet the increasing cost of maintenance expenditure. Keeping in view these factors in consideration a proportionate amount of funds required by the Universities and the Colleges for the development of Libraries is arranged by the central government through the UGC. Governance of Indian University (1971) a study brought out under the Chairmanship of Dr. P.B. Gajendragadkar, has mentioned "the finances of a university are almost entirely provided from public funds, the tuition and examination fee paid by students do not amount, in general, to more than a quarter of the total budget. The Committee strongly recommended that the UGC should be involved effectively in advising to the State Governments is determining the quantum of maintenance grants. Without adequate financial resources, for more than those currently provided, and above a certain minimum critical level, there can be no progress in higher education, except marginally here and there. The UGC, with the intimate connection with all Indian University should advise and assist them in upholding the dignity of the university education system. It should act as guide, philosopher and friend of the university system. Thus the future of the university educational progress will depend largely on the dynamic role of the Commission (UGC). To make proper distribution of its development grants, the UGC takes opinion of the experts time to time on the proposals made by the universities and colleges. The visiting committee consists experts of various fields taken from the university system. The State Government representatives are also associated in order to involve State Government in development programmes of Universities. The Commission as per the direction of its act enquires about the financial needs of the University Libraries. It gives guidelines or sands visiting committees in the beginning of the plan. On receipt of requirements and recommendations of the committees pattern of grant allocation is decided. These exercises are made before the commencement of five year plans and a considerable grants are made available for the development of university and college libraries. Previously, temporarily funds were also received by University Libraries from Ford Foundation, Rocke Feller Foundation and PL-480 funds for a period of time.

The main problem concerning library resources is that the additional inputs provided by the UGC for the purchases of books and journals are not supplemented by other sources. Since the library system is the heart of the university education system, it would be desirable for the UGC to suggest to the states to treat expenditure on additional journals subscribed during a plan period and procurement of text books or books prescribed as necessary reading as part of maintenance during the next plan period.

The number of universities every year are approaching to the UGC for allocation of additional funds for their libraries. Due to heavy increase in the cost of books and journals especially in science and technology subjects that to published in foreign countries the funds have become insufficient for subscribing to those journals which were being subscribed in the previous session. The UGC has noticed this problem which almost common in all the University libraries. The problem of subscribing new titles of journals which are added to cover up the new trends of the subjects and also to add latest published good books is very alarming in all university libraries.

To overcome on this problem co-operative plans named Library

Regional Centres, National Information Centres and INFLIBNET (Information and Library Networking) vide which through electronic medium all the University Libraries will be able to share information from the agencies which are collaborated in the programme is prepared. The latest INFLIBNET schemes is debated intensively and placed before the planning commission for consideration.

Pattern of Central Assistance

The first effort in this direction was the recommendations of Education Commission (1948-49). The Commission while making its recommendations for raising the standards of teaching and research realised that the university and college library facilities are very poor and annual grants are inadequate. It recommended that annual grant for University Library should be 6.25 per cent of the total budget of the university or Rs. 40 per student. A special non-recurring grant should be made available one's in five year to cope with the arrear of books and journals which are not covered in regular fixed allocations. Special grants for the purchase of manuscripts may also be provided to the university libraries.

The UGC, since its inception (1956) is being arranging substantial grants for building up university libraries. It follows liberal policy in recommending funds for alround development of libraries. It pays development Grants both to the Central Universities and State Universities. The maintenance grant to Central Universities is paid by the UGC where to the State Universities by the State Government. The calculations to decide the grants are made by the UGC itself. The college which fulfil the UGC guidelines also receives grants. The ratio/pattern of grant is decided on the regular reviews made by the UGC. The amount made available vary from institution to institution due to variation in their strength, facilities, infrastructure, income and various other such factors.

In UGC efforts, first Dr. C.D. Deshmukh the Chairman UGC realised the vital role of grants in development of libraries. He was very much aware that the grants made available by the UGC were not adequate to meet the requirement of Building, Equipment, Collection Building and Services etc. A special grant of four crore was made available with the formulation of the "Committee for the Development of University and College Libraries, (1965)" under the Chairmanship of Dr. S.R. Ranganathan with following members to advice UGC on library matters.

Dr. S.R. Ranganathan (Chairman)
Shri S. Bashiruddin
Shri S. Hingwe
Shri B.S. Keshwan and
Shri S. Parthasarathy

The UGC Chairman while inagurating the work of the Committee in 1958 said that the UGC attaches great importance to the efficient running of libraries. The Committee made a survey of Selected University libraries and worked out details and submitted its chief recommendations as on annexure 2.1 which was accepted by the Commission (UGC) in its meeting held in the month of June, 1959. The Committee recommended for

(i) The UGC's functions in the establishment and development of university and College Libraries, and
(ii) Guidance of University and College Libraries.

Pattern of grant has been reviewed periodically. The Education Commission 1964-66 realised with ever increasing enrolment in Universities and Colleges, the demand for library services has been constantly growing. Unlike the past the library staff have now to cater to the diversified needs of undergraduates, post-graduates and research scholars, it was stressed that modern University libraries are also required to serve a larger number of Academic departments and to perform new functions like Indexing and Abstracting. To meet these requirements, the present position of expenditure on books and periodicals is not satisfactory! The Education Commission (1964-66) therefore, made following recommendations:

(i) "The utilisation of Library grants should be suitably phased over a plan period. In other words, there should be a regular programme of strengthening of Academic departments and the library, instead of haphazard overfeeding them in one year and starving them in the next.
(ii) About 6.5 per cent of the educational budget as reasonable expenditure on libraries. This could vary from 6.5 per cent to 10 per cent depending on the stage of development of each

university library. A university should spend each year about Rs. 25 for each student registered and Rs. 300 per teacher.

(iii) The foreign exchange needed for University and College Libraries should be allocated separately to the UGC".

The Parry Committee Report (1967) recommended Universities should devote a minimum of 6 per cent of their income to their libraries.

In 1975 to link education more closely to the development of the country and to achieve ideals of socialism, secularism and democracy, basic grant of 242 lakhs was provided to Universities and deemed to Universities to purchase books and journals.

During the fifth plan period "the UGC to ensure an integrated view of library development, provided grants for construction/extension of Library Buildings, purchase of books and journals, library furniture, reprography and for essential library staff. The grants were made available to every college affiliated to a University eligible to receive grants from the Commission (UGC). Some basic grants for the purchase of books, text books, and other reading materials was provided. These grants ranged from 10,000 to Rs. 40,000 depending on the enrolment. During 1979-80, a sum of Rs. 77.35 lakhs was paid to colleges as basic grants for the purchase of books and journals. In allocation of funds high priority was accorded to libraries during Vth plan 1974-75 to 1978-79. The allocation in respect of 12 universities appeared in UGC Review Committee Report (1981) Rs. 399.28 lakhs gives an idea of the range of grant distribution. The amount was at higher side then the previous plan allocation of Rs. 123.32 lakhs only.

Review Committee on Social Works Education (RCSWE) (1981) recommended for additions to the library and the minimum financial assistance suggested was Rs. 20,000 per 100 students and at least 500 major titles a year plus journals. Where an undergraduate programme is added to a graduate programme, the expenditure should be provided for at least 800 titles a year and 40 journals. Five year development grants should be given to libraries of Institutions which receive state government grants, similar to the UGC pattern. It was also noted that state Institutions need special inputs both for development grants for libraries and enhanced expenditure on the regular library grants.

The Working Committee on Central Universities (WCCU) (1984) while studying library facilities noticed that due to the increased cost of books and the same time reduction in the library grants to the

Universities, teachers experience considerable difficulty in getting the latest books. Committee recommended to provide higher allocations to the Universities for library books and journals. Keeping in consideration recommendations of various committees. "National Policy on Library and Information Systems advocated for adequate financial support for the development of libraries and Information Systems. The national as well as state governments should provide an expenditure of 6 to 10 per cent of their education budgets for the libraries. All Educational Institutions should similarly provide for their own libraries 6 to 10 per cent of their total budget".

Additional Allocations to Universities and Colleges for development of libraries, beginning from the year 1987-88 has been provided as per norms given below:

1.	Universities/Deemed to be Universities with Ceiling of normal development grant of Rs. 100 lakhs and above.	Rs. 10 lakh each
2.	Universities/Deemed to be Universities with Ceiling below Rs. 100 lakhs	Rs. 7 lakh each
3.	College	Rs. 25,000 each

The Association of Indian Universities study results reported in National policy on University libraries, library expenditure for books, periodicals and bindings averaged was 33.8 per cent. The mediam was 36.5 per cent. The standard library budget suggested is between 30-35 per cent for books periodicals etc.

For inviting the fresh proposals for development programmes during a plan period UGC recommended following pattern of Assistance

Sixth Plan (1980-85)

Library Staff	100%
Equipment for Library Services	100%
Books and Additional Journals	100%
Library Buildings	50%

The UGC provided Seventh Plan Guidelines to invite Proposals

Keeping in view the resolutions of the NEP (1986) and PAO (1986) to create a capable Society which can face challenges and problems of the present and future, as usual practice the Universities were requested to prepare their proposals on these lines. On receipt, the proposals were discussed with the Senior University faculty members and State Government officials for arriving at the pattern of grant to be allocated during the plan.

The NEP resolved that higher education should become dynamic as never before. The necessary dynamism will consist of the following:

(i) Consolidation and Expansion of Institutions,
(ii) Development of Autonomous College and Department,
(iii) Redesigning Courses,
(iv) Training of Teachers,
(v) Strengthening Research,
(vi) Improvements in Efficiency,
(vii) Creation of Structure for Co-ordination at the State and National Levels, and
(viii) Mobility.

UGC's policy, therefore, have three main aims:

(i) Improvement of standards and quality of education;
(ii) Restructuring and diversification of courses; and
(iii) Removal of disparities and regional imbalances in higher educational facilities.

To achieve these objectives the UGC revised the guidelines for purchase of books and journals including strengthening of Book Banks etc. guidelines, it was suggested that assistance for development of Postgraduate Education in College may be extended to the department subscribes to at least 5 standard academic journals in the subject.

The College while formulating proposals for development during the Seventh Plan were advised to include proposal for books and journals including setting up of Book Banks and or augmenting facilities in the existing Book Banks with a view to augmenting the facilities and improving reading habits among the students. Before fresh allocations UGC also seeks information on expenditure on books and journals for the department in the past year under the following heads:

(a) Non-recurring, if any
(b) Recurring
(c) Number of journals subscribed with titles and amount of subscription per annum.

Assistance Programme for College Developments

In the light of POA of NEP (1986) the need of restructured relevant courses was very much felt as a result of it, vocational subjects, advanced diploma programmes and degree programmes were included in selected colleges during Seventh plan. It was also realised that the College Education is an important area in Higher Education in particular in our country where majority of students study for higher education in the colleges. Another reason may be the college provides education in rural or backward areas of the country. To fulfil the financial needs of the colleges the UGC circulates guidelines in the beginning of every five year plan. The UGC policy for development of college during Seventh plan was based on following three aims:

(i) "Improvement of Standards and Quality of Education;
(ii) Restructuring and diversification of courses; and
(iii) Removal of disparities and regional imbalances in higher educational facilities".

To achieve these objectives the UGC made assistance which includes purchase of Books and Journals and strengthening of Book Banks. In seventh plan guidelines colleges were advised to propose 20 per cent of the total grants for Books and Journals. The following Pattern of Basic Assistance was made during Seventh plan period.

Books and Journals including Book Banks	100%
Professional Staff for Library	100%
Audiovisual Equipment	100%
Building including extension of Library Buildings	50%

Eighth Plan (1990-95)

1. Library Staff	100%
2. Equipment : Reprography	100%
3. Books and New Journals	100%

4. Library Building 100%
5. Machinery and Equipment 75%

For academic and other staff under faculty improvement of twenty per cent to twenty-five per cent grants for creating new posts can be used for supporting professional staff.

The UGC guidelines suggested 45 per cent to 50 per cent allocations be available for library equipment. The parametres have been suggested to decide the departments to receive library assistance.

The UGC suggests criteria for selecting university departments in the developed and developing category. In the case of developing departments increasing inputs are made available with in the plan allocation to bring up their facilities and activities to an optimal level essential and for their teaching and general research work and for maintenance of adequate standards. In Annexure IV of the guidelines the library facilities are regarded as an important variable. The following guidelines are available to decide assistance:

(i) Over 2000 titles (multiple copies of the same book to be taken as one title,
(ii) All average of 100 new books added each year,
(iii) At least 20 journals currently subscribed and with back volumes for past 20 years or so.

Suggestions for Deciding Assistance

While considering financial assistance, the criteria for such support should base on the following:

(i) Size of the library
(ii) Strength of the students
(iii) Strength of the staff
(iv) Strength of the library users
(v) Number of faculties available
(vi) Number of special academic schemes
(vii) Nature of the collections
(viii) Objective of the library
(ix) Services in operation such as references service, Select documentation service, current awareness service, Indexing and abstracting service, Reprographic service, Bibliographic

service, Computer search service etc.

(x) Increasing number of publications
(xi) Increasing cost of the documents
(xii) Technological applications
(xiii) Use of non-book materials
(xiv) Future programmes.

The financial supports are of two type i.e. (1) Recurring and, (2) Non-recurring.

1. Recurring Grants are generally for purchase of books and journals, maintenance of regular services and anticipated expenditure to meet the salary of the staff.
2. Non recurring grants are provided for specific purpose i.e. construction of library building, purchase of furniture and other equipment and *ad hoc* grants to meet special requirements. Under non recurring grants UGC has been giving grants to Universities for construction of new library buildings as well as for renovation or extension library buildings. Despite of Recurring, Non-recurring, *ad hoc* grants, State funds and extraordinary other financial sources are chased to meet the requirements. The libraries are under budget crisis, reason for which may be the following:

(1) Visiting team of the UGC in absence of library experts does not make proper assessment,
(ii) Increasing price of books, journals and equipment etc.,
(iii) Increasing salaries,
(iv) Multidisciplinary expansion,
(v) Development of new faculties,
(vi) Enrolment growth,
(vii) Technological application,
(viii) Unplanned expansion of the department/organisation to which it belongs,
(ix) Unplanned retention of unserviceable library collections, and
(x) Lack of library culture in using funds.

The aim of the UGC is to assist the university and college libraries to function more effectively in raising academic standards and encouraging research work. The important initiatives of the UGC can be studied in the following captions.

(a) Grant allocations for construction or for renovation of library buildings and other equipment – reprography and computers.

(b) For collection development

Book Banks
Purchase of Books
Purchase of Journals
Purchase of Non-Book Records.

(c) Quality improvement programme

Revision of Pay scales and qualifications
Summer courses,
Training courses,
Seminars etc.

Keeping in view the funding provisions, the seminar (1986) on the subject held at Osmania after taking into consideration phenomenal rise in the number of users of University libraries, number of books and journals being published as mentioned and their price rise, the seminar recommended 20 to 25 per cent of the total budget of the university may be set apart for the operation grant of University libraries. It also recommended the annual increase in the budgetory provisions of Universities libraries shall be the order of 15 to 20 per cent in keeping with the general price rise.

Inspite of all efforts financial constraints are always there. One of the most important reason in India is speedy academic population, multidisciplinary knowledge expansion and technological revolution. The 1980s was a decade of remarkable progress in the information field and a new era of electro books, electronic mail and non print book material has emerged. Throughout the world government and non-governmental agencies are producing non-book material for future use.

With the statutory responsibility of maintenance of standards the UGC is contributing for the growth and development of such material in the university libraries.

Suggestions

– While making annual allocations the UGC should use the

experience of librarian.

- For all round development of libraries the librarian should have first line status/rank to know the requirements of the Institutions.
- The collections should be developed on some systematic plan or on the objectives of the host department/organisation i.e., university/college.
- The collections must contain all forms of recorded information.
- The allocations should be based on the objectives of the library.
- The services should be taken in consideration.
- Sufficient provisions should be opened for new innovations and technologies.
- The concept that library is a growing organisation should be taken in its full spirit.
- The expenditure on libraries should not be linked with the present day need, it should have future needs in its planning.
- The resources should be worked out on a national policy.

3

ALLOCATIONS FOR INFRASTRUCTURE

Assistance for Construction or for Renovation of Library Buildings

Since its inception the UGC has paid attention to inadequate building facilities available in University Libraries and considerable Grants were provided to construct new library buildings or to renovate or to expand existing facilities during five year plan developments. Because the "Building from an integral part of development as effective utilisation of grants for additional Staff, Equipment, Books and Journals can not be ensured unless these are linked with the minimum building requirements". The grants were provided in development programmes on a sharing basis, which was utilised by a good number of libraries. As reported in the UGC annual report during Second and Third plan period Rs. 2.67 crores grants were paid. Similarly on the recommendations of Fourth plan visiting committees Rs. 78.88 lakhs were allotted. Under India Wheat Loan Educational Exchanges Programmes of United States of America a grant of Rs 54,30,000.00 was provided for building expansion of five libraries. The grants reported in UGC project study, for building purpose by Universities is as on Annexure 3.1. Up to March, 1973 UGC sanctioned Rs. 3,83,75,289.00 for library buildings. About two third share was from the UGC.

Inspite of all these efforts, it is a pity that most of the University and College library buildings are inadequate to meet the growing needs of the present day libraries what to talk of their future plans. It is therefore, suggested that UGC should initiate efforts to decide national policy to extend national resources or central support on per capita basis for construction or renovation of library buildings. While considering proposals local variation, Institution's capacity, objective and future plan should be given due waitage. The expenditure involved for building purpose in total should be born either by Central

Government i.e (UGC) or by State Government. There should be liberalised rules to set up co-ordination and to fix up the share of these two bodies. The ratio/pattern of grant and allocations should be reviewed time to time to overcome the market fluctuations in price of building material and involved labour cost etc. The need of space in library buildings and equipment installation requirements is under rapid change. Now the age has come when libraries has to be airconditioned to preserve non book material and sophisticated electronic machines.

The UGC Review Committee (1981) conducted a survey and reached to the results as on Table 3.1. The study reveals that the facilities available in reading rooms were inadequate to meet the growing requirements of users. The information was called from 12 Universities and following observation were made.

TABLE 3.1: Reading facility in Twelve Selected Universities alongwith Percentage of Students who can get seat in Library

Name of University	No. of Students	No. of reading seat in Library	% of Students having seat in Library
Poona	2,773	300	11
Sardar Patel	1,220	700	57
Jadav Pur	1,197	400	33
Calicut	791	325	41
Shri Venkateswara	1,798	432	24
Madras	2,508	290	12
Gauhati	1,844	210	11
Calcutta	13,057	702	5
Ranchi	1,590	40	3
Punjab	4,801	500	10
Gorakhpur	7,362	100	2
Delhi	9,738	400	4

University and College Library Development Committee (1965) studied the subject in its gravity first time and devoted forty-one pages to discuss existing infrastructure, equipment, location of various sections of the library, rooms, doors and windows. Even use of solar heat for users, moisture affects for collections was taken in notice. The Committee was conscious for the book protections and the Chairman of the Committee Dr. S.R. Ranganathan requested Indian Standard Institute to establish a Sectional Committee on Library Buildings, fitting and furniture. The Committee finalised first standards for the purpose 15:1533–1960 entitled "Code of practice relating to primary elements in the design of library building".

The standards for the library buildings, fittings and furniture established by the Indian Standards Institution and extracted in Chapters N and O of Ranganathan Committee was proscribed for all the University and College Libraries. It was recommended that any proposal, for a new buildings, fittings and furniture, or for the adaptation of existing buildings, or for its extension for library purposes should be examined and approved by a library expert appointed by the UGC.

Later these Standards were revised and the latest approved standards are as on Annexure 3.2.

In Seventh plan proposal guidelines laid down for Universities the UGC has suggested that Universities may spend up to 20 per cent of the ceiling of grant for construction of building requirement for library facilities. It is also conscious of the fact that standards of Higher Education in India has great concern with Colleges. In fact 85 per cent undergraduate students 14 to 15 per cent of the research students are enrolled in colleges. The 55 to 60 per cent of the allocations, therefore, be available for purpose of equipment required for libraries to provide for reprographic and other facilities in colleges.

The document has suggested to provide following information to consider the proposals.

(i) "Do you have a Central library of the University? If Yes, how many persons can use the Reading Room facilities at a time,

(ii) Do you have reprographic facilities (State microfilm, Xerox, Ammonia Print .... etc.) in the library, and

(iii) Whether the library is airconditioned or not".

Eighth Plan guidelines pattern of assistance for library building was 50 per cent.

For Equipment and library books and journals, "the remaining 45 to 50 per cent of the allocation indicated would therefore, be available equipment required for library to provide for reprographic and other facilities Audio-visual Aids, VCR, VCP, overhead projectors etc. and for purchase of library books and journals for the central library as well the library services to give especial support to some of the specific academic programmes of teaching and research".

Reprographic Equipment and Services

In 1974, the UGC first realised the need of strengthening a few University libraries in different regions. The idea was to create facilities is the institutions fall in that region. In the programme reprographic facilities and microfilm etc. were provided to facilitate the information users. Further on the advise of the Standing Committee on Measures for Strengthening University and College Libraries the UGC, in April 1981 accepted the following recommendations:

> "Universities may be permitted to acquire, where necessary, a reprographic Unit out of the library grants allocated by the Commission during the Sixth plan. However, if the total expenditure to be incurred for this exceeds Rs. one lakhs, the proposal may be sent to the Commission for prior Concurrence".

The UGC made clear in Seventh Plan guidelines 55 to 60 per cent allocations would be available for equipment required for research and for library to provide reprographic and other facilities and to support on going programmes of teaching and research.

The UGC has brought out a report to extend computer facilities for human resource development at universities and college, 1990; for Eighth plan projections. The Committee has recommended to initiate computer related courses in Library Science.

4

COLLECTION DEVELOPMENT

The MHRD annual report part I, 1989-90 has mentioned that the "Books play an important role in the field of education. In the present contest when their is an expansion of education facilities all round in the country, the demand for books in terms of quality as well as variety of subject has been increasing, the book promotion. Division of the department of education has a number of schemes and activities which aim, inter-alia, at promoting the production of good quality books at reasonable price, encouraging indigencous authorship, promoting the reading habit and providing assistance to the Indian book industry in its problems". To carry out the Govt. policy as well as to maintain the standards of higher education the UGC has also initiated number of programmes for providing good quality books to the university and college students and teachers.

The world of books is very wide and there may not be any one who has not experienced the holy spirit of the books. Every book leaves its impression on menkind in its own way. The *Ramayana, Bible, Kuran, Gurugranthsahib* and on the other side the Mandal Commission Report are the few popularly known examples. As a result of it through the ages the generations are preserving books for their posterity.

History

The history of collection development in University libraries has its roots in the birth of these libraries. The University libraries consists all type of publications collected through gifts, donations, exchanges and purchases etc. Collections are huge in number and may include published books, manuscripts, dissertations, reports published or unpublished, project reports contributed by the scholars of various disciplines etc., in some cases the collections of individuals received as donations. In early days library collections were recognised as assets and were symbol of status. As a result book on various disciplines were retained by the collection builders. These were consisting book or non book forms. Main collections of university libraries consists books and journals and developed through purchase or sometimes in exchange or gift. The present collection growth in almost in all the University libraries is in an unplanned manner. With modernised library services and experience it has been realised that only working collections should be retained in libraries. The collection should be adequate to the need of the teachers, students and scholars.

The Ranganathan Committee (1965) recommendation and Government of India, Ministry of Finance Order No. F.23(7) E-II(A) 83 dated Feb. 7, 1984 has given direction to deal with obsolete or undesirable publications. The University system has number of varieties such as the universities are of various type — State University, Central University and Deemed to be universities and similarly colleges are of Govt. and affiliated which receive central grants for library collection development under various schemes from Central and State Government. The beneficiaries are 39,47,922 students, 54,973 teacher and a large number of research scholars who are spread out throughout the country. The strength, area of study, number of facilities and on going programmes of the universities effects the collections. If the university to which the library belongs has number of schemes such as Department of Special Assistance, large number of research projects and various centres, then it will naturally get more central funds for its collection development. Since the universities are doing for research and teaching, a good number of publications are developed by the researchers and teaching staff itself, even then the collections of university libraries are not satisfactory.* Cooperation, therefore, in library services is realised and with electronic technology and computer application, efforts are being made to share the resources of a group of libraries. Networks based on various criterias have been planned such as DELNET, CALIBNET, INFLIBNET etc. In near future, through automation university libraries system will be able to make intensive use of the collections of those libraries which are under the network programme. Thus the progressive thinking has linked the size of the library with intensive

* The Seminar on National Policy on University Libraries held at Osmania University in 1986 noticed "that libraries are not acquiring even one per cent of the total world output of reading materials at present. This is so even with regard to the learned journals"

use i.e. with efficient library services. The programme will also generate new records to improve the collections.

The Universities have no policy that how many books will be added to the library or to a particular departments or subject. However, the funds available are distributed among the various departments as a result of which in one subject more books of less price are added at the same time in other subjects costly few books only. Similarly in some subjects Governments reports and the assignment reports are developed in large number where in some subjects such developments are not taking place. Keeping all these variations suggestions were made in all the times to provide adequate funds to purchase good books and journals. Unfortunately "there is no formula for estimating with precision how much money a university should invest in its libraries or on collection building. Though the University Education Commission (1948-49) had suggested about 6.5 of the total educational budget as reasonable expenditure on libraries and the Education Commission (1964-66) suggested that, as a norm, a university should spend each year about Rs. 25 for each student enrolled and Rs. 300 per teacher. The figures would be much higher to-day in view of the rise in cost but above all that present position of the total expenditure on books and Journals is far below the norms suggested by the Education Commissions.

"In addition to having departmental and Seminar libraries it stated with a working collection of books and Journals the Central Library should facilitate inter disciplinary communication and also the work of research scholars in borderline disciplines. An adequate collections of carefully selected and well organised books are essential. The book selection should be oriented towards supporting instruction and research. In fact even a comparatively small collection of sensitively chosen books may work wonders in the life of students. The teaching and library staff should determine the titles and copies of books to be purchased and periodically work together to discard obsolete books. Many of these can be replaced with microfilms and micro-cards." But inspite of all these recommendations the condition of library collection is miserable. Latest developments of non-book form will widely effect the future collection growth of the University Libraries.

Measures taken by the UGC

The UGC since its establishment providing grants to the universities for the purchase of books and Journals under general development schemes as well as in some special programmes such as Centres of advance study, Departments of special Assistance, Departmental Support, Support for research to individual teachers and to group of teachers and research improvement programmes etc. For general development, grants are allocated to the central library as well as departmental libraries.

Ranganathan Committee (1965)

The gravity of the subject was very well recognised by the University and College Libraries Development Committee (1965). The Committee was of the view that the book selection should be regulated by some policy which may be lay down by authority concerned. The Committee made recommendations as an Annexure 4.1 for purchase of reading materials. It also recommended to enhance assistance to purchase book and journals. The following separate recommendations for departmental collections were made.

"A post-graduate department of a university may be allowed a permanent loan of upto a maximum of 2,000 volumes that are expected to be frequently needed for the research in progress in the department.

This does not apply to the books whose duplication has been made especially for the use of the department".

The volumes on permanent loan may be kept in the department for an indefinite period. As and when the needs of the department change, the volumes no longer required in the permanent loan collection may be returned to the Central Library and new volumes taken in their place.

The volumes in the permanent loan collection are subject to recall by the librarian at his discretion in case they are wanted for other readers or for technical purposes.

Besides the permanent loan, each department may be given a temporary loan of up to 100 volumes, returnable only in the last week of the term or the year as may be prescribed.

Copies of text-books, if any, supplied to teachers for teaching purposes should be independent of loan of even kind and should be treated on a par with the material equipments furnished to a teacher.

Current issues of periodicals should be kept on display in the periodicals rack of the Central Library for one or two weeks to give a chance for everybody to peruse them and released for loan to research workers only after that period.

It is not economical to build independent departmental libraries, unless a department is far away from the campus. It will unnecessarily add to the load of responsibility of head of the department. Even in the case of a department having its own library for reasons of distance or other reasons all impersonal work such as book-purchase, classification, cataloguing and binding of books should be left to the care of the Central Library."

A study conducted by the UGC appeared in Standards of University Education Report (1965) presents an analysis about the use of library books by the teachers and students as on Annexure 4.2 for thirty universities. One week library use or issue of books has been shown with number of variables to visualize the justification of the expenditures incurred on the purchase of books in every plan.

The UGC Review Committee (1977)

The committee realised that with an ever increasing enrolment in universities and colleges, the demand for books and journals has been continuously growing. Unlike in the past university libraries have now to cater to the diversified needs of under-graduates, post-graduates and research scholars. As a result of which allocation to books and journals were very high during the period 1974-75 to 1978-79 in comparison to previous plan as appeared in Review Committee Report (1981). Allocations of 12 universities were Rs. 399.98 lakh where during Fourth plan it was 123.32 lakh as on Table 4.1 and 4.2.

The study also shows the level of expenditure on books and journals is far below the norms suggested by the Education Commissions. The main problem concerning library resources is that the additional inputs provided by the Commission (UGC) are not supplemented by other sources. It would be desirable to the Commission to suggest to the states to treat expenditure on additional journals subscribed during a plan period and text-books or books prescribed as necessary reading part of maintenance during the next plan period. Steps should also be taken to avoid unnecessary duplication in the acquisition of books and costly journals and particularly foreign journals.

TABLE 4.1: Developmental Assistance on Books and Journals during 1969-70 to 1973-74 Fourth Plan

(*Rs. in lakhs*)

University	Amount allocated	Amount utilised
Sardar Patel	6.00	3.40
Jabalpur	3.35	3.35
Poona	13.00	11.29
Sri Venkateswara	10.06	10.02
Calicut	13.41	13.41
Madras	10.23	9.30
Punjab	19.98	19.75
Gorakhpur	9.20	9.19
Delhi	3.50	3.50
Ranchi	7.15	6.88
Calcutta	14.57	14.22
Gauhati	12.87	5.82
	123.32	110.13

TABLE 4.2: Development Assistance on Books and Journals during 1974-75 to 1978-79

(*Rs. in lakhs*)

University	Amount allocated	Amount utilised
Sardar Patel	15.00	15.00
Jabalpur	22.00	22.00
Poona	24.30	24.30
Sri Venkateswara	24.45	24.27
Calicut	36.55	36.55
Madras	42.05	31.83
Punjab	53.68	51.98
Gorakhpur	21.90	15.18
Delhi	28.40	24.66
Ranchi	16.45	16.45
Calcutta	65.40	63.02
Gauhati	49.80	31.09

The UGC Review Committee (1981) concluded that "book banks have not made a uniform impact in all the universities and colleges. There are certain gaps in implementation. However, there is an obvious need to continue this programmes.

According to UGC Study Collection Position on March 1989

The libraries in 179 universities and about 5,500 colleges in India have a fairly large collection of documents developed over the years. A conservative estimate, based on the analysis of the questionnaires received from the university libraries, gives the total collection of all the university libraries together as 3.5 million documents. Out of them about 2 million documents include text books, monograph, reference books, manuals, maps and atlases, conference proceedings, theses, scientific and technical reports, serials, etc. Some university libraries have also standard specifications, patents, and other special materials. No print material such as micro-flims, micro-fiche and other audio-visual forms are available in many libraries. A number of university libraries have a good collection in old manuscripts, palm leaves, hand written texts, tamrapatras and calligraphic historical and religious texts. Some precious rare books are also held by libraries. The collection in the libraries is in various languages. While the predominant collection may be in English language, the Indian language publications, more particularly in arts and humanities fields account also for the collections in university libraries. The languages of the region in which the university is located, gets a favoured treatment in collection development. In addition to 14 official languages, Pali, Sanskrit, Persian, Arabic, etc. are covered by the language collection of university libraries.

Inspite of all this enormous growth of documents and limited resources, it is not possible to any institution to collect each and every thing which is brought out by the age. Similarly classification, cataloguing and professional services for each paper is not possible. Some steps, therefore, are needed to assess all such documents. While considering collection, present services and future potentialities should be taken in consideration. To keep balance in demand and resources, what is to be added to the collections is very important. Acquisition is the major activity of the library. Even than no serious attention has been paid to this exercise. Unplanned and undefined procedures of collections and literature production has resulted in haphazard growth.

There are various other reasons also responsible for the unpresidential haphazard growth. The foreign reminders entered to Indian market. Some of the Indian traders are also after money and producing many substandard publications. There are no norms for selection. The recommendations of the expert are ignored due to time gaps in utilisation of funds. To face all these situations attention should be paid to production, quality, contents and selection to make best use of the resources. The experience of the Librarian should be utilised in book selection. The scientists, scholars and students should be encouraged to take interest and to participate in book selection. There may be central approval policy or central acquisition body to select purchase. At least eighty per cent publications should be recommended by the central authority rest of the 20 per cent may be left on the local need basis. In any case the acquisition should not be unplanned and individualistic manner as it is in operation now. The users help should not be ignored in any case for proper utilisation of the sources.

For adequate purchase the present discount practice should be reviewed and if possible abolished to bring down the prices of the publications. Side by side policy for pricing the publications should be effectively implemented by the Central Government. The library collections should have a collective approval instate of individualistic approach. The public funds should be invested on public patterns.

As estimated by the INFLIBNET about 150 crores is being spent every year on the collection of books and journals. The cost of books and journals published both in India and abroad is raising day by day and it becomes extremely difficult for a university/college to maintain the current level of subscription inspite of increase in the allocation for books and journals by the funding agencies. While it is ideal to equip the libraries in the Institutions so that they are self-sufficient to cater to the needs of the academic community, in view of the huge expenditure involved on higher education.

The books and journals of the libraries are purchased on the advise of the University or College Library Committee. Which scrutinises the requirements sent to it by various departments. Pooled purchase is made through the Central library to fulfil the requirements of the departmental libraries. The Purchase Committees recommendations should be followed to make effective use of limited resources.

The Commission (UGC) before commencement of a plan period on receipt of the proposals from Central Universities, State Universities and Colleges which fulfil the guidelines laid down by it decides the pattern of assistance to be allocated to the Institutions keeping in view their future academic programmes. The assistance provided by the UGC and appeared in UGC assisted project for First to Fourth plan period is as on Annexure 4.3.

Pattern of Assistance

As, per Seventh plan guidelines 50 to 60 per cent of the allocations were provided for purchasing of library books and journals for Central library as well as for the departmental libraries required to support the ongoing academic programmes of teaching and research. The grants to be paid during the plan period are as on in Eighth plan guidelines for the universities for purchases of books, 100 per cent assistance provisions is made. The Commission has made allocations for the Eighth plan to state universities as on Table 4.4.

"Highly Technological and information based modern society has in many respects strong impact on the educational systems. Knowledge is increasingly becoming the power base for individual and groups of individuals. It is substituting inherited wealth and to a large extent social background as a springboard for individual career and status. In the information oriented society a highly trained executive is more effective than a stock owner. The countries of technological world are regarded as an advanced.

TABLE 4.3: Seventh Plan Grants for Books and Journals

(Rs. in lakhs)

University	Grants Utilisation on 31.3.90		Special Assistance Outside plan
1	2		3
Agra	12.45		7.00
Allagappa	17.00		—
Allahabad	38.00		10.00
Annamalai	30.00		—
Anna	14.00		—
Bangalore	24.30		10.00
Berhampur	23.00		—
Bhavnagar	5.00		—
Bharthiar	25.00		—
Bharathidasan	15.00		—
Bombay	8.00		10.00
Burdwan	9.21		10.00
Baroda	15.00		10.00
Calcutta	16.00	11.00	10.00
Dibrugarh	10.00		10.00
Garhwal	3.50		10.00
Gauhati	17.17	13.00	—
Goa	5.00	2.50	—
Gujarat	26.00		10.00
Gulbarga	25.00		10.00

(Contd.

TABLE 4.3 (*Contd.*)

1	2		3
Guru Nanak Dev	10.00		10.00
Himachal	6.00		10.00
Jadavpur	18.50	18.00	10.00
Jammu	26.00	17.00	10.00
Jodhpur	14.00		10.00
Kalyani	5.99 (Basic Book) +	3.00	10.00
Kanpur	10.00	7.00	7.00
Karnataka	19.00	16.00	10.00
Kashmir	6.50		10.00
Kashi Vidyapeeth	15.00		7.00
Kumaun	13.50		10.00
Kurukshetra	16.00		10.00
Lucknow	26.00	22.00	10.00
Madras	15.00	13.00	10.00
Madurai Kamraj	28.00		–
Maharshi Dayanand	17.00		–
Manglore	15.00		10.00
Manipur	9.47		10.00
Marathwada	10.00		10.00
Meerut	20.00	14.00	10.00
Mohan Lal Sukhadia	16.00		10.00
Mother Teresa Women's	10.00		–
Mysore	23.00		10.00
Nagpur	12.50	10.50	10.00
North Bengal	16.00		–
Poona	14.20	9.00	10.00
Punjab	20.00	17.00	10.00
Punjabi	19.50	19.00	10.00
Rabindra Bharati	15.00		10.00
Rajasthan	15.00		10.00
Roorkee	20.00		10.00
Sambal Pur	16.60		10.00
Sanskrit Vishwavidayala	7.50	2.00	7.00
Sardar Patel	25.00	15.50	10.00
Saurashtra	19.65	19.64	10.00
Shivaji	15.00	14.00	10.00
Shri Jagannath Sanskrit	3.00		–
S.N.D.T. Women's	11.40	6.85	10.00
South Gujarat	21.00		10.00
Tamil	40.50		10.00
Tripura	10.00	9.50	–
Utkal	15.00		–
Vidyasagar	15.00		–

Source: Eighth Plan Development proposals and recommendations New Delhi, UGC, 1990.

TABLE 4.4: Allocations as UGC Share for Purchase of Books and Journals Recommended during Eighth Plan period.

(Rs. in lakhs)

University	Total allocation for Eighth plan	Allocation for the year 1990-91
1	2	3
Agra	25.00	5.00
Alagappa	20.00	5.00
Alcahabao	42.00	15.00
Andhra	26.00	10.00
Annamalai	44.00	10.00
Anna	17.00	5.00
Awadesh Pratap Singh	15.00	5.00
Bangalore	35.00	10.00
Barkatullah	35.00	5.00
Bchrampur	32.00	5.00
Bhagalpur	30.00	5.00
Bharthiar	30.00	5.00
Bharatidasan	25.00	5.00
Bihar	30.00	5.00
Bhavnagar	25.00	5.00
Bombay	30.00	5.00
Burdwan	40.00	7.50
Calcutta	40.00	10.00
Calicut	35.00	5.00
Cochin	30.00	5.00
Devi Ahilya	30.00	5.00
Dibrugarh	30.00	7.50
Dr. Hari Singh Gaur	35.00	7.50
Gauhati	30.00	7.50
Goa	55.00	10.00
Garhwal	27.00	10.00
Gujarat	45.00	5.00
Gulbarga	30.00	5.00
Gurughasi Das	20.00	8.00
Guru Nanak Dev	30.00	10.00
Himachal	30.00	2.50
Indra Kala Sangeet	8.00	2.50
Jadavpur	35.00	7.50
Jagan Nath Sanskrit	10.00	3.00
Jammu	30.00	10.00
Jiwaji	28.00	10.00
Jodhpur	40.00	5.00
Kakatiya	18.00	5.00
Kalyani	30.00	5.00

(Contd.)

TABLE 4.4 (*Contd.*)

1	2	3
Kaneswar Singh	12.00	2.00
Kanpur	15.00	5.00
Karnataka	35.00	10.00
Kashmir	25.00	10.00
Kashi	15.00	7.50
Kerala	45.00	10.00
Kumaun	35.00	5.00
Kurukshetra	35.00	5.00
L.N. Mithila	25.00	5.00
Lucknow	45.00	10.00
M.S. University	35.00	5.00
Madras	40.00	5.00
Madurai	37.00	5.00
Magadh	40.00	5.00
Mahatma Gandhi	25.00	5.00
M.D.	35.00	5.00
Manglore	30.00	5.00
Manipur	20.00	10.00
Marathwada	30.00	5.00
Meerut	35.00	5.00
Mohan Lal Sukhadia	30.00	5.00
Mother Teresa	13.00	5.00
Mysore	35.00	10.00
Nagarjuna	15.00	5.00
Nagpur	30.00	5.00
North Bengal	35.00	7.50
Osmania	37.00	5.00
Punjab	50.00	10.00
Patna	30.00	5.00
Poona	35.00	5.00
Punjabi	30.00	10.00
Rabindra Bharati	35.00	5.00
Rajasthan	35.00	5.00
Ranchi	30.00	5.00
Rani Durgavati	45.00	10.00
Ravi Shankar	27.00	5.00
Roorkee	35.00	10.00
Sambalpur	30.00	5.00
Sampurnanand	9.00	2.00
Sardar Patel	35.00	5.00
Saurashtra	30.00	5.00
Shivaji	30.00	5.00
SNDT.	30.00	5.00
South Gujarat	30.00	5.00

(*Contd.*)

TABLE 4.4 (*Contd.*)

1	2	3
Shrikrishna Devaraya	26.00	5.00
Shri Padmavati Mahila	20.00	5.00
Sri Venkateswara	45.00	5.00
Tamil	25.00	5.00
Telugu	13.00	3.00
Tripura	23.00	10.00
Utkal	20.00	5.00
Vikram	35.00	5.00
Vidya Sagar	20.00	5.00

The Information Science has over the last few decades emerged as a key subject area in education. The teaching is increasingly will depend in near future on the Information stored on non book materials. New devices such as CD-Rom etc., have emerged even in the present century as a means to make information dissemination more efficient and faster than ever before. The Seminar on National Policy on University Librarians (1986) also recommended "Universities should also be encouraged in enriching their audio/video and microfilm collections. University may also be advised wherever feasible to go in for microfilms, particular in respect of journals with a view to avoiding duplication and thereby reducing costs both in acquisition and space". In this direction UGC has made considerable efforts by establishing EMRCs and AVRCs to develop non-book form to support country wide classroom programmes. To meet the urgent need and to improve the situation, of the rapidly and the steeply escalating prices of books, journals etc., and increase in the number of books and journals being published and the growing incapacity of libraries to buy as many of these as may be relevance to the teaching and research programmes in the campus, the Seminar on National Policy on University Libraries (1986) recommended the following –

(a) "To build up the collections of the libraries in so comprehensive and complete manner as to enable them to be responsive to the scholarly needs of the academicians in the country.

(b) To husband the limited financial resources so that a mighty reservoir of knowledge and information required by the country is built up and the limited funds are thus made to go a long way."

It is well accepted that "the 1980 was a decade of remarkable progress in the field of information and it was also a period of great turmoil for library profession at large. Secondary publication begin to disappear in printed form as terminals became common place of storage and access costs continued to decline. New reference books emerged both in the form of electro-books and in the form of data banks accessible on line. Many existing references books were converted from print on paper to electronic form." The development is still continuing and proving a revolution in information generation.

Thousands of data bases has been created world wide for storing several types of information on numerous subjects access to these databases is provided globally by on line service. To interconnect these services "number of networks are coming in existence. Such services are not much popular or in easy approach to Indian users. With the introduction of International Gateway Pocket switch service in Dec., 1988 the cost involvement is reduced to a great extend. Videsh Sanchar Nigam has made agreement with telebase system Inc. to work as mediator with Indian users to over come the problems of foreign currency payment. Thus the rates are regulated at national level to make the information use more popular in Indian users.

The Government has reviewed its 'book import policy' under new import policy. Under the New Import Policy (1988-91) import of educational, scientific and technical books/journals is allowed under Open General Licence (OGL) Teaching aids such as microfilms and microfiches with or without readers-cum-printers film strips/slides with or without audio cassettes/video tapes of educational nature can be imported under OGL by recognised educational scientific, technical and research institutes, Centre and State Government departments, etc. Dealers with a turnover of Rs. 3.00 lakh or more are eligible to apply for import licence on the basis of 10 per cent of their purchase turnover for books other than those covered by OGL.

The collection building in its total perspective is the joint adventure of Government and the users. The Central Government through UGC provides assistance under various schemes which in brief we are discussing afterwards. At the same time users also develops collections through their writings. In collection development, teachers and students has given too much contribution by way of writing books and articles and dissertations. The total number of publications added by the university sector are not known. It is continuous process for making the comprehensive working collections in modern age, sufficient mechanisation should be welcomed. The automation efforts will not only save the space and money but also increase tremendous speed and efficiency in communication of the information.

The UGC Schemes under which Financial Assistance has been Provided for Books and Journals

(i) *India Wheat Loan Educational Exchange Programme*

Under India Wheat loan programme (PL-480) funds were received by the UGC during 1954-60. Out of which grants were given for purchase of books and journals and for extension or renovation of selected libraries.

(ii) *Book Banks*

The Commission (UGC) as accepted the fact that the good text books generally are very costly and remains beyond the reach of the common students. It was therefore, decided in 1963-64 to provide grants on cent-per cent basis to strengthen the book banks in all the disciplines. The objective of the scheme was to provide books to needy and deserving students for study on long term basis. The universities were directed to make use of fixed portion of the grants given by the UGC for establishing Book Banks. For starting the scheme grant of Rs. 10,000 to degree colleges and Rs. 15,000 to post-graduate colleges was made available. Earlier to 1985 assistance was provided on the basis of strength based categories. But after 1985 assistance was calculated at the rate of Rs. 60 per student subject to a maximum of Rs. 50,000 to a college in a plan period. Thirty per cent of the UGC library grants were allowed to utilise for book banks. The assistance provided by UGC on the scheme is as on Table 4.4a. The programmes was especially launched for the welfare of poor students.

(iii) *Low Price Books*

In consultation with the UGC and the Ministry of Social Welfare and culture a programme for reprinting of books on low price editions, which originally published in foreign countries and are of use to the university and college students was initiated by the Government through National Book Trust (NBT). In this scheme the UGC's role was only to get books evaluated from the subject experts available in the academic institutions. These efforts promoted library collections as well.

TABLE 4.4a: **The UGC Assistance under Quality Improvement for Book Banks during 1969-70 to 1982-83**

(Rs. in lakhs)

Year	Amount	Total
1969-70	–	
1970-71	–	
1971-72	114.13	
1972-73	23.68	
1973-74	9.91	
1974-75	58.14	
1975-76	96.44	
1976-77	75.19	
1977-78	46.19	
1978-79	18.37	
1979-80	–	
1980-81	–	
1981-82	1.52	
1982-83	–	295.05

Source: UGC RC (1981).

(iv) *Regional Library Centres*

Since independence the efforts have been made to link up education more closely to know all round developments of the country. To achieve the objectives in 1976, in Vice-Chancellors Conference with educational issues, development of library facilities was widely debated and the Commission (UGC) was of the view, besides strengthening libraries in the universities and colleges some centralised facilities for libraries on regional basis should be developed. To set up such Regional Library Centres (RLCs) a committee was set up by the UGC in 1976. The Committee recommended to set up four centres at Calcutta, Bombay, Bangalore and Banaras and National Centre at Delhi. The centres were to provide most efficient information facilities like reprographic, microfilm and mechanised services through computers at minimal cost to entire university system, and research establishments. The information stored in the region was for the use of the libraries of that region. The centres were to functions as the part of the central library of the University. Grant allocation of sixty thousand and 7 core staff to each centre was proposed in Fifth plan. Two crore sanction was made in Fifth plan period. The programme was reviewed in Sixth plan and regional library centres which were state wise were taken up as UGC National Information Centres (NIC). Three such centres have been established and details of which can be seen under NIC studies on page 93.

(v) *Study Centre*

The UGC planned to introduce study centres with appropriate Library Services during the Fourth Five Year Plan period. Recurring and non-recurring grants were provided to the selective study centres to have multiple copies of books, non-recurring grant of Rs. 20,000 for books to existing centres and 30,000 to new Centres and Rs. 10,000 for staff and furniture, recurring grant assistance of Rs. 10,000 for staff salary and Rs. 3,000 for contingency was made available. During the year 1979-80 a grant of Rs. 5.60 lakhs was paid to 16 universities and prior to this during 1977-78 to 23 universities Rs. 44.91 lakhs were paid under the scheme.

(vi) *Committee for Strengthening of Infrastructure in Science and Technology (COSIST)*

The Commission launched a scheme on strengthening of infrastructure in Science and Technology on a highly selective basis to raise their standards comparable to their counterparts elsewhere in the developed countries. Till the end by the year 1988-89, 98 departments were supported under the scheme. Under this scheme grants for book and journals were provided as on (Table 4.5). The scheme will continue in Eighth plan to identify new departments for support. The scheme is to brought out qualitative improvement in teaching at the undergraduate level.

Commission in 1974-75 extended programme to the Humanities and Social Science i.e. COHSSIP. It was to bring improvement in teaching and learning at the under graduate level.

(vii) *Restructuring of Courses*

The scheme of restructuring of courses was initiated by the UGC during the Seventh plan period to make education relanent to the needs of the community. Up to March, 1989, 9 universities and 136 colleges has introduced restructured courses. In 1986 a number of Curriculum Development Centres (CDC) have been set up. The scheme is to review the existing syllabi and to suggest measures for modernising unit model courses. The efforts will make education socially relevant and meaningful. As on March, 1989, 27 CDC were in operation. Model curricula for 20 disciplines has been developed and are in discussion with Commission for implementation. Under the scheme funds were provided for arranging books and journals as on Table 4.6 during the last plan period. In 1990, the curriculam development committee on the recommendation of UGC Panel on Library and Information Science has been set up in U.G.C. to modernise the curricula of Library and Information Science.

TABLE 4.5: The UGC Assistance for Books and Journals under COSIST Programme during 1985-86 to 1989-90

(*Amount in Rs.*)

Year	Universities	Colleges
1985-86	5,70,000.00	2,10,000.00
1986-87	14,63,968.95	—
1987-88	5,48,718.00	30,000.00
1988-89	19,54,915.45	30,000.00
1989-90	25,67,691.61	30,000.00

TABLE 4.6: The UGC Grants under the Scheme Restructuring of Courses for Purchase of Books during 1985-86 to 1989-90

(*Amount in Rs.*)

Year	Universities	Colleges
1985-86	87,000.00	4,19,700.00
1986-87	20,000.00	9,27,500.00
1987-88	1,30,000.00	9,40,601.00
1988-89	—	9,46,595.89
1989-90	40,000.00	4,31,000.00

(viii) *Computer Facilities*

The Commission (UGC) has been providing financial assistance to universities for setting up computer facilities and computer centres since 1984-85. Up to 1988-89, 104 universities were covered under this scheme. 481 colleges were also selected to extend the facility. Under the scheme assistance for books and journals was made available as on Table 4.7. The scheme and assistance is periodically reviewed to meet the market requirements.

TABLE 4.7: **The UGC Grants provided under Computer Facilities Scheme for Books and Journals**

(Amount in Rs.)

Year	Universities
1984-85	1,10,000.00
1985-86	4,71,908.00
1986-87	2,85,000.00
1987-88	88,361.80
1988-89	1,51,000.00

The UGC has approved a operational plan for the development of computer facilities in university and colleges at a financial outlay of Rs. 52 crores during the Eighth Five Year Plan period. Facilities also extended to impart training in computer use. It is also considering to allocate a substantial amount for library books and journals to meet the purchase of computer and such other requirements.

(ix) *Scheme for the Development of Engineering and Technology*

The Commission has been providing financial assistance for books and journals to strengthen engineering departments especially during the year 1988-89. Thirty-five universities were provided assistance. Assistance given for books during last ten years is as on Table 4.8.

(x) *Centres of Advanced Study*

"The Commission has been providing special assistance since 1963 to some promising departments in humanities, social sciences and science and technology subjects in the universities, carefully selected on the basis of their work reputation, existing facilities and potentiality for further development to function as Centre of Advanced Study (CAS). These centres are intended to encourage the pursuit of excellence, and to improve quality and raise standards at the post-graduate and research level. Each such centre is a part of university where it is located. The grants made available to the scheme for books and journals during last five years as on Table 4.9. There were 41 centres up to March 1989 in all disciplines. The Centres have all India nature of promoting mobility in the country.

TABLE 4.8: The UGC Assistance for Books and Journals under General Development Scheme of Engineering and Technology in the Universities

(Amount in Rs.)

Year	Universities
1980-81	18,59,000.00
1981-82	83,06,980.00
1982-83	30,60,000.00
1983-84	47,15,000.00
1984-85	21,88,976.00
1985-86	40,76,165.03
1986-87	54,05,610.64
1987-88	1,53,40,500.00
1988-89	60,69,921.65
1989-90	1,00,43,292.97

TABLE 4.9: The UGC Assistance on Books and Journals under Quality Improvement Programme for Strengthening Centres of Advanced Studies

(Amount in Rs.)

Year	Universities	Colleges
1980-81	N.A.	N.A.
1981-82	80,000.00	N.A.
	43,042.59	
1982-83	1,84,000.00	N.A.
	60,772.27	
1983-84	75,000.00	54,831.00
1984-85	1,55,000.00	
1985-86	1,05,000.00	50,000.00
	10,55,000.00	—
1986-87	5,45,000.00	53,808.00
	10,40,000.00	10,500.00
	50,000.00	—
1987-88	85,000.00	1,00,000.00
	1,55,000.00	—
1988-89	1,63,551.00	25,000.00
	13,50,000.00	—
1989-90	—	75,000.000

(xi) *Department of Special Assistance*

The programmes was initiated in 1982-83 as a support to quality programme to strengthen and consolidate teaching and research. There were 169 DSA programmes were in operation up to March, 1989. The UGC assistance for books under the scheme was provided as on Table 4.10.

TABLE 4.10: The UGC Asistance for Books : Departments of Special Assistance

(Amount in Rs.)

1981-82	6,27,013.24
	4,064.42
1982-83	8,25,900.83
1983-84	12,62,023.59
	18,816.62
1984-85	6,35,515.04

Department Research Support (DRS) scheme was started in 1978. 72 DRS were in operation up to March 1989. The support for books and journals for the centres was provided by the UGC as on Table 4.11.

TABLE 4.11: Assistance on Books and Journals under Quality Improvement Programme for Strengthening Selected Deptts

(Amount in Rs.)

Year	Universities	Colleges
1980-81		
1981-82	3,50,000.00	–
1982-83	2,02,600.00	–
1983-84	2,25,000.00	–
1984-85	3,35,000.00	–
1985-86	3,35,000.00	1,10,000
	17,52,343.75	20,000
1986-87	6,30,000.00	1,50,000
	11,72,500.00	–
	1,60,000.00	–
1987-88	1,74,000.00	
	27,33,614.00	20,000
	2,10,000.00	–
1988-89	6,24,500.00	–
	7,16,380.46	–
1989-90	4,85,000.00	–
	15,80,000.00	–

(xii) *Bio-Technology*

A collaborative programme has been in operation since 1985-86 between the Department of Bio-technology. Govt. of India and the UGC for strengthening teaching and training in Bio-technology on a selective basis in Universities which have active research groups in the field. Six universities were identified for the purpose which have been conducting M.Sc./M.Tech. courses in bio-technology since then. The Department of Bio-technology gives financial assistance for books and journals. The funds provided by the UGC for books and journals during five years as on Table 4.12.

TABLE 4.12: Assistance provided for Books and Journals under the Bio-technology Improvement Scheme

(*Rs. in lakhs*)

1985-86	—
1986-87	1,00,000.00
1987-88	1,00,000.00
1988-89	—
1989-90	—

(xiii) *Research Projects*

The Commission provides assistance to the teachers, undertaking research or learned works in their fields of specialisation. The projects are of two categories: minor and major. Minor projects are short term research projects. The financial assistance provided up to the ceiling of Rs. 15,000 by the Commission. Every sanction includes a handsome amount for purchase of books and journals. In the year 1988-89 237+906 (Humanities, Social Science & Science) such projects were approved. Major projects may be undertaken by individual or by a group of teachers or by a Department as a whole. These are projects for long-term interdisciplinary studies. Every such sanction of major projects also includes grants for purchase of books and journals. During the year 1988-89 136+199 major projects in different disciplines were approved. The figure for the UGC assistance made under the programme for books and journals are not available. However, as on Table 4.13 separate allocations were also made to strengthen the science, social sciences and humanities under the quality improvement programmes.

TABLE 4.13: **The UGC Assistance for Books and Journals for Departmental Research Support**

(Rs. in lakhs)

Year	Universities	Colleges
1985-86	70,000.00	40,000.00
1986-87	4,45,000.00	—
1987-88	6,85,000.00	3,15,000.00
1988-89	2,40,000.00	—
	1,57,916.67	—
1989-90	2,75,000.00	—
	2,99,810.00	—

(xiv) *Subject Panels of Experts*

The Commission constitutes once in every two years, panels of experts in various subjects of study and research from the universities and other institutions, to advise it on all matter relating to present status and standards of teaching and research in the subject concerned, facilities, available within the country and in different regions for teaching, training and research in the subject and also to suggest measures to be taken for further development of facilities to promote studies at an advanced level. These subject panels periodically review syllabi and courses of study followed by different universities at under-graduate and post-graduate level with reference to such courses of study being made up-to-date and, wherever necessary, relevant to the regional and national needs and also to bring about necessary inter-disciplinary aspects. The advice given by the panels has helped in initiating appropriate measures to achieve required standards of teaching and research in the subject concerned. The terms of reference for various subjects panels are laid down to guide the work of the panels.

As a body of experts in a subject area and related discipline and interdisciplinary fields, and coming from universities, R&D laboratories and other institutions, which are assisting the Commission in continuously reviewing the activities of the different universities in education and research, and in suggesting suitable measures and methods for improvement of standards and relating education to emerging national needs. The panels are also giving expert advice for support of research by identifying thrust areas of importance and by way of evaluation and monitoring of research projects, within the overall policy of the Commission. The subject panels while suggesting various measures for raising the standards through strengthening infrastructure also recommend collection development in all disciplines, the scheme is under review. The comments are available in the form of discipline reports.

TABLE 4.14: The UGC Assistance Provided to Purchase Books Under the Scheme of Development of Humanities and Social Sciences

Year	Rs.
1980-81	91,11,000.00
1981-82	1,60,97,229.14
	53,614,84.00
1982-83	1,29,06,369.66
1983-84	4,04,00,723.02
1984-85	1,36,78,449.23
1985-86	2,42,00,611.63
1986-87	2,27,89,170.00
1987-88	1,53,25,000.00
1988-89	1,06,77,940.00
1989-90	2,33,35,000.00

TABLE 4.15: The UGC Assistance Provided to Purchase Books under Scheme Development of Science Scheme

Year	Rs.
1980-81	69,68,000.00
1981-82	1,09,30,016.02
1982-83	75,38,447.39
1983-84	3,54,74,000.00
1984-85	1,44,82,500.00
	30,000.00
1985-86	1,41,84,000.00
1986-87	1,09,48,827.00
1987-88	91,26,000.00
1988-89	87,85,000.00
1989-90	68,83,000.00

(xv) *Film Study Centre*

The film study centres has been set up in selected universities and colleges. A UGC Cell is set up at the national Film archives of India, Pune and 22 universities/colleges have been selected for establishing such centres. Under the scheme assistance for books and journal was provided as on Table 4.16.

TABLE 4.16: The UGC Assistance provided for Books and Journals under the Film Clubs Scheme

(*Rs. in lakhs*)

Year	Universities	Colleges
1985-86	65,500	–
1986-87	6,00,000	4,00,000
1987-88	1,00,000	–
1988-89	–	–
1989-90	2,21,400	–

(xvi) *Mass Communication*

The electronic devices like television and radio are used to promote education even in the rural areas of the country. For this purpose well structured teaching material is prepared by the outstanding scholars in the various disciplines. The communication infrastructure of the country which has very rapid expansion is utilised. The UGC through the 'countrywide classroom programme', is imparting high quality university level education even to the remotest parts of the country. The programme is telecasted for two hours daily through INSAT 1B at the Doordarshan Network. The medium is English at present. To make programmes more effective colour TV sets have been provided to a number of institutions. The following audio-visual research centres (AVRC) and four Educational Media Research Centres (EMRCs) have been set up by the Commission. In first instance for the distance learning material is to be produced in 15 subjects in the form of audio-video cassettes. The Commission has taken up a project "Non broadcast mode Educational Material." A number of programme like workshops, awards and exhibitions have also been organised to make services more effective. The Commission has offered Rs. 25 lakh as special assistance to Calcutta University to develop equipment for mass communication studies.

A. The Commission (UGC) at present has following Educational Media Research Centres (EMRCs)

(i) Jamia Millia Islamia, New Delhi.

(ii) Gujarat University Ahmedabad
(iii) Poona University, Pune
(iv) Central Institute of English and Foreign Language, Hyderabad.

B. Audio-visual Research Centres (AVRCs)

1. Osmania University, Hyderabad
2. Roorkee University, Roorkee
3. Jodhpur University, Jodhpur
4. Anna University, Madras
5. St. Xavier's College, Calcutta
6. Madurai Kamraj University, Madurai
7. Kashmir University, Srinagar
8. Punjabi University, Patiala
9. Manipur University, Imphal
10. Devi Ahilya Vishawavidyalaya, Indore

The approach of the UGC through this programme is to reduce disparities among regions to develop knowledge and communication system to promote development efforts. Therefore, in Seventh Plan it puts emphasis on 'Mass media like radio, audio-visual aids and TV to take education more effective to the community as well as to supplement classroom teaching programmes for students of the whole nation.

The telecasting of these programmes commenced with effect from 15th August 1984. So far about 2,000 programmes have been produced. To coordinate the work of these centres and effective use of their production, the UGC has planned to establish a Audio Video Library at JNU campus, New Delhi. The Library will be equipped with adequate computer facilities. The UGC assistance provided in last five years on the scheme for books and journals is as on the Table 4.17.

TABLE 4.17: The UGC Assistance provided for Books and Journals under the Mass Communication Centres Scheme

(Rs. in lakhs)

Year	Universities	Colleges
1985-86	–	–
1986-87	–	–
1987-88	76,02,834.80	5,58,886.00
1988-89	–	–
1989-90	–	–

The UGC has estimated that the various mass media print and audio visual and allied areas of mass communication, with an over all expected growth rate of 8 per cent, will create job opportunities for some 75,000 young professionals in the next five years. The scheme worked out for Eighth plan prospective on journalism/communication education in India undersection C has kept a provision of 0.25 crores for books and journals for centres of excellence for 11 departments and also 0.75 crores for other 40 departments. It also has provision for 0.35 and 0.70 crores provisions for library technical staff etc.

(xvii) *National Information Centres*

After reviewing the Fifth plan scheme of Regional Library Centres in Sixth plan under research improvement programmes UGC National Information Service Centres have been established to provide up to date information in the areas of interest. The objective of centres are to improve the information access to the teachers and research scholars and also to provide bibliographic support in their respective disciplines. The centres provide current awareness and references service. So for the UGC has set up the following Information Centres to cover major disciplines.

Subjects	Institutions
Science	Indian Institute of Science, Bangalore
Social Science	M.S. University, Baroda
Humanities	S.N.D.T. Women's University, Bombay

National Science Information Centre, Bangalore was set up in 1983 and since then working under the guidance of a programme committee. The centre has a total number of 287328 profile and abstracts has been generated for 3795 users. The centre provides on request full length photocopies of the current papers. It has implemented computer to streamline the services. The Centre also runs a training programme of one year duration.

National Information Centres in the field of Humanities and social sciences were set up one each at SNDT University, Bombay and M.S. University, Baroda. The SNDT Centre covers disciplines: Sociology, Home Science, Library Science, Special Education, Women's Studies, Gujarati, while M.S. University, Baroda Centre covers Economics, Political Science, Education and Psychology. The centres are suppose to provide bibliographic data and documentation in the respective disciplines. The centres have started developing computer data base to extend Current Awareness Services (CAS) and reference service. UGC assistance provided under the scheme is as on Table 4.18.

TABLE 4.18: Assistance provided for Books and Journals under the Library Information Centres Scheme

Year	Amount
1980-81	–
1981-82	6,00,000.00
1982-83	–
1983-84	–
1984-85	5,00,000.00
1985-86	–
1986-87	–
1987-88	–
1988-89	–
1989-90	6,00,000.00

(xviii) *Area Study Centres*

"Under this programme the Commission has been providing assistance to selected universities for undertaking in depth studies relating to various aspects of different countries and regions of the world particularly of those with which India has had close and direct contacts." The assistance covers strengthening of library facilities also. The Universities are getting assistance for development of 16 areas. The scheme is under review.

(xix) *Preparation of University Level Books by Indian Authors*

The Commission provides financial assistance to university system outstanding academics and scholars for preparing high quality books, monographs and reference books etc. Under this scheme 1035 projects were approved and 352 manuscripts have been completed up to March 1989. The scheme is under review. Under the scheme during 1985-86, to universities 4.87 lakhs and to college 1.45 lakhs assistance was provided.

(xx) *Journals*

The Commission continued to support publication of quarterly journals in Physics Education, Mathematics Education, Biology Education and Chemistry Education, Journals in English or regional languages brought out by the departments. A grant of Rs. 1.6 lakh was paid to universities for this purpose during 1988-89.

(xxi) *Books*

The Commission has a scheme of Text book writing. Paucity of text books and teaching material suited to Indian conditions is very much realised. The UGC has taken steps to remove it by commissioning a number of specialists to write suitable books. The press institute of India, Indian Institute of Mass Communication, the Publication division, National Book Trust, UGC media centres, UGC Publication Unit, under the UGC schemes a good number of useful books has already developed. It was initiated with the idea that Indian text books written by Indian authors will be suitable to Indian needs.

(xxii) *Publication Grants for Quality Works*

The UGC provides support under publication grants as on Table 4.19 to universities for publication of learned research work including doctoral thesis. The works under this scheme for assistance only within a period of ten years after its submission are considered. In this scheme university may utilise a sum not exceeding 15 per cent of the allocation in the head. The proposals from the college teachers and other scholars who have been awarded Ph.D. Degree may be invited and may be got evaluated by two experts other than the examiners. The amount of subsidy for publication of a thesis should not exceed Rs. 7,500 unless the University is itself publishing on its own, in which case it may meet actual expanses. It also coordinates various other similar funding agencies such as ICHR, ICSSR, NBT and Indian Institute of Advance Studies, Simla. The main intenstion behind the scheme is to improve the quality of the publications to improve the quality of library services as well.

To persue scientific career in undergraduate level the UGC has a programme named as College Science Improvement Programme (COSIP) while designing the programme attenstion was paid to 'expenditure on library service' and 'Production of books'.

TABLE 4.19: The UGC Assistance under Quality Improvement Programmes for Publication of Thesis and Learned Research Work

(Rs. in lakhs)

Year	Amount
1969-70	0.78
1970-71	0.85
1971-72	1.57
1972-73	2.87
1973-74	2.60
1974-75	3.69
1975-76	2.88
1976-77	8.23
1977-78	9.78
1978-79	10.66

Writing of books/publication of research work

(Amount in Rs.)

Year	University	College	Scholar
1980-81	—	—	7,905.00
1981-82	2,29,742.11	1,32,108.65	1,000.00
1982-83	4,66,290.95	37,500.00	—
1983-84	4,61,889.37	99,756.79	4,700.00
1984-85	9,97,089.44	Publication of Journals	
	64,659.75		
	1,92,418.36	62,801.29	2,200.00

The changes which are taking place, in the university education are putting close impact on the library collections. In fact in most of the cases there is no relevance between collections of libraries and the nature of their services or with teaching and research programmes of the host institutions/universities and colleges. Nineteenth Century technological revolution and slogan 'education for all' has increased the use of books. The requirement of students and researchers includes wide area of special reports, standards, patents, monographs and other such qualitative publications. The variety of information has evolved specialised services such as bibliographies, documentation, reprographic and translation services. The collection have been affected by the increasing involvement of students and teachers. New knowledge has emerged in the form of new disciplines. Even all these developments the libraries which are heart or central of university education system has not equipped with priorities.

While considering collection building future programmes should be kept in view as well as present needs. There should be a national policy and also policy of every library to keep the functional collections. To meet the requirements the book budget has been increased in many folds even than funds are ineducate and not proportionate to the published documents. Especially the subscription amount of periodicals has gone very high. Due to the reason the libraries has suspended buying many good journals. The problems are common in almost all university libraries. The following measures may be suggested to solve the problem. While deciding collection policy should taken care of

- New subjects
- New syllabai
- Enrolment growth,
- Number of books emerging to the field
- Resources
- Infrastructure available to process.

There are number of constraints in the process of collection building:

- Inadequate financial resources
- Non availability of sound selection policy
- Non availability of good books
- Unplanned development
- Irrelevant collection of reports and back volumes
- Ratio of books and uses is not systamatic
- Costly reference books
- Costly selection books such as books in print etc.

For smooth collection development and for effective use of resources the following steps have been taken during the past years.

- Good offices committee is circulating conversion rates of foreign currency and general terms of supply
- The foreign exchange is made available by State Bank or by any other Bank according to the provisions of RBI manual
- The books are taken out from the store items and calling quotations is discontinued by the Government of India

- To improve collections weeding out provision are made
- Special grants are provided to meet the arears
- Fairs are arranged to give publicity to the new titles
- New technology and computer application has increased use of information quantum.
- Computer application in internal working has improved the collection development.
- The resources sharing scope with Net Works has increased the quantum of information records for their users.
- The steps are taken to provide control and assistance in time to cope with the situation.

In the report of the committee to enquire into the working of the central universities. Observations, it is accepted that a university provides learning opportunity and books in libraries to students and scholars. The committee made observation that due to increased cost of books and reduction in the library grants to the universities, teachers experience considerable difficulty in getting the latest books. The suggestion was made to make high allocations for library books. The UGC arranges recurring and non-recurring grants for Central universities. Under the provisions assistance as on Table 4.20 was made for the purchase of books and journals. The assistance for purchase of books and journals as on Table 4.22 was also provided to the constituent/affiliated college of Delhi university during the last five years.

TABLE 4.20: Development Grants to Universities (1969-70 to 1973-74) for Books and Journals

(*Rs. in lakhs*)

1969-70	167.92	
1970-71	140.66	
1971-72	96.96	
1972-73	127.24	
1973-74	115.62	648.40 Total
1974-75	153.35	11%
1975-76	212.59	
1976-77	342.31	
1977-78	356.63	
1978-79	536.08	1610.96 Total
		23%

Source: UGC RC (1981).

TABLE 4.21: Grants to Central Universities Under Subplan for Books and Journals

(*Rs. in lakhs*)

	1985-86	1986-87	1987-88	1988-89	1989-90
AMU	2.00	1.00	10.00	1.50	4.00
BHU	—	13.00	15.00	—	—
Delhi	14.00	3.00	24.50	—	30.00
Hyderabad	25.65	—	30.00	0.02	10.00
JNU	13.00	—	20.00	6.00	—
NEHU	—	12.00	—	—	—
Visva Bharati	2.00	—	25.00	—	—
Pondicherry	—	5.00	20.00	—	3.00

TABLE 4.22: Grants paid to Constituent/affiliated Colleges of Delhi University for Books and Journals

(*Rs. in lakhs*)

	1985-86	1986-87	1987-88	1988-89	1989-90
1	2	3	4	5	6
Hamdard	2,500.00	—	—	—	—
Lakshmibai	80,000.00	50,000.00	1,20,000.00	—	—
Ram Lal Anand	5,000.00	—	50,000.00	90,000.00	—
I.P. College	75,000.00	—	1,65,000.00	55,000.00	—
Kamla Nehru	46,250.00	—	25,000.00	40,000.00	1,65,000.00
Kirorimal	45,000.00	—	2,00,000.00	—	75,00.00
Maitreyi	60,000.00	—	25,000.00	1,10,000.00	1,50,000.00
Moti Lal Nehru					
(Day)	35,000.00	—	25,000.00	—	—
(Evening)	50,000.00	—	25,000.00	—	50,000.00
Shri Ram College of Commerce	24,500.00	—	1,65,000.00	—	—
Desh Bandhu (Day)	95,000.00	25,000.00	90,000.00	70,000.00	—
(Evening)	50,000.00	50,000.00	—	—	—
School of Correspondence course	20,000.00	—	—	—	—
Bharati Mahila	—	26,000.00	25,000.00	50,000.00	—
Guru Govind Singh	—	22,8000.00	1,25,000.00	—	—
Institute of Home Economic	—	35,460.00	1,65,000.00	—	—
Jesus Marry	—	50,000.00	1,00,000.00	20,000.00	20,000.00
Satayawati (Day)		50,000.00	25,000.00	—	1,80,000.00
(Evening)	—	50,000.00	25,000.00	—	—
Shri Arvindo (Day)	—	36,000.00	25,000.00	20,00.00	1,25,000.00
(Evening)	—	—	—		1,50,000.00

(*Contd.*)

TABLE 4.22 (*Contd.*)

1	2	3	4	5	6
Shyam Lal (Day)	—	50,000.00	—	—	2,00,000.00
(Evening)	—	8,420.00	—	—	25,000.00
Swami Sharadhanand	—	50,00.00	75,000.00	—	1,80,000.00
College of Vocational Studies	—	50,000.00	25,000.00	1,75,000.00	—
ARSD	—	50,000.00	25,000.00	5,000.00	—
Daulat Ram	—	59,900.00	1,25,000.00	50,000.00	—
Hans Raj	—	50,000.00	1,00,000.00	1,60,000.00	25,000.00
Hindu	—	50,000.00	25,000.00	1,40,000.00	—
PG DAV (Day)	—	50,000.00	75,000.00	20,000.00	25,000.00
(Evening)	—	37,000.00	25,000.00	20,000.00	—
Rajadhani	—	13,867.00	2,15,000.00	2,10,000.00	—
SGTV Khalsha (Day)	—	50,000.00	74,212.00	25,000.00	—
(Evening)	—	50,000.00	25,000.00	—	—
Shaheed Bhagat Singh	—	50,000.00	—	25,000.00	—
SPM College of Women	—	23,000.00	25,000.00	25,000.00	—
Vivekanand Mahila	—	50,000.00	95,000.00	25,000.00	—
Zakir Hussain (Evening)	—	50,000.00	95,000.00	—	—
Dayal Singh (Day)	—	13,000.00	2,32,000.00	—	—
(Evening)	—	50,000.00	—	20,000.00	—
Miranda House	—	15,000.00	1,05,00.00	—	79,998.38
Kalindi	—	—	1,00,000.00	35,000.00	—
Ram Lal Anand	—	—	25,000.00	42,360.00	—
(Evening)	—	—	—	—	1,25,000.00
Jankidevi	—	—	50,000.00	70,000.00	—
Gargi College	—	—	25,000.00	62,500.00	—
Shyam Lal (Day)	—	—	25,000.00	—	—
(Evening)	—	—	25,000.00	—	—
Lady Irwin	—	—	25,000.00	—	30,000.00
Lady Shri Ram for Women	—	—	25,000.00	1,10,000.00	1,35,000.00
Mata Sundari	—	—	25,000.00	—	—
Ramjas	—	—	25,000.00	—	—
Shivaji	—	—	1,65,000.00	50,000.00	—
Shaheed Bhagat Singh (Day)	—	—	25,000.00	—	—
Shri Venkateswara	—	—	3,00,000.00	75,000.00	75,000.00
St. Stephan's	—	—	50,000.00	—	1,25,000.00
Zakir Hussain	—	—	25,000.00	1,85,000.00	—
Gargi	—	—	—	—	1,00,000.00
Uni. College of Medical Sciences	—	—	—	—	10,00,000.00
Delhi College of Arts and Commerce	—	—	—	—	25,000.00

5

QUALITY IMPROVEMENT PROGRAMMES

There is well established expansion in every sphere of libraries. It may be holdings, campus population, number of faculties departments and sections, library buildings, number of extension libraries, branch libraries, including of new various library services, application of modern technology, research and library culture etc. It has invited attention of the policy-makers to search suitable management to these unites. The important challenge with the library development is to keep pace with the objectives of its main body or department to which it belongs, while planning it should consider its campus population and physical and financial resources. Then only the management can expedite effective services to provide right information to right user at the right time, which is the goal of the library services.

For effective and intensive use of libraries recommendatory bodies 'Library Committees' were formulated under University Act. With the formulation of Library Advisory or Recommendatory Committee the working of librarians is not independent even though the committee in almost all cases is a part of host organisation. In some cases this provision effects adversely when librarian is not associated in any capacity to the committee. The librarian who is an employed professional, scholar and administrator should be made responsible to plan policies, organise services and to create resources. The approach will increase efficiency in service. The Advisory Committee will frame policies on library matters.

The University and College Libraries are for academic cause and suppose to work as Communication and Research Centre. These preserve knowledge in the form of human spirit. The libraries, therefore, are recognised treasure house of knowledge. Even then during pre-independence period much attention was not paid to their development. It is only after independence as we have mentioned "UGC has given priority to the integrated development of library facilities in the universities and colleges". Leading personality Shri

V.K.R.V. Rao expressed "more important than classroom and good teachers, is the availability of books and periodicals. Their accessibility of far effective use by well trained and motivated library staff is also important for enabling not only the dissemination of knowledge among the student community, but also for the stimulation of creative impulses in their thinking". Thus libraries regarded as an important means of promoting the communication and advancement of knowledge. It has become an inseparable part of academic programmes in institutions. The need, therefore, of professionally qualified personnel to run libraries efficiently was very well felt even in the middle of this century.

Standards of Education (1965) demanded "The library should have adequate and well qualified staff. Each library requires several grades of employees. At the top well be a men of the calibre of a University professor who has especialised in some aspect of library science, after having done a full degree course and who has capabilities for organisation and management. In the next grade will be his deputies who will lookafter different sectional activities of the library like cataloguing, reference work, reading room management, etc. Than finally there must be numerous assistants helping in all activities from the accessing to the issuing of books. The top man must have a qualification corresponding to a Doctorate in Library Science or in any of the discipline; the Deputy Librarian should have obtained degrees, after undergoing training at a university, while the other assistants should possess diplomas, the courses for which extend over at least one year. We must have at least one university centre in each province offering facilities for training for the diploma courses". To make the libraries centres for research, attention should be paid to reference service. Lectures and tutorials must be supplemented by work in the library. Properly qualified library professional can help student and teachers in locating the readings of their subjects. Trained staff can provide bibliographic and documentation services. Reason for scientific research and socio-economic development of the country has resulted modern school of library and information science in about eighty one University departments. The discipline is emerged as a new science for studying an art of information storage and dissemination.

The University Libraries has various categories of the library staff which includes professionals, semi-professionals and non-professionals etc. The Commission (UGC) to meet the qualitative expansion and to maintain standard of services recommends certain measures and inservice programmes for maintaining the quality of Staff. University and college library Development Committee (1965) suggested number of steps to improve the conditions.

The Committee realised that, the Academic qualifications of the library staff should be at par with those of the professors, the readers, the lectures and the tutors. But the library staff must be able to speak the language of the academic community. In fact, librarians and professors should work partners in a co-operative academic enterprise. This is now fast becoming the accepted practice in the universities all over the world. India cannot stand outside this world-trend. It was also realised that apart from general academic qualifications of a high order, the libraries professional staff should also have professional qualifications of an equally high order.

The (1965) Committee report recommendation of qualifications and grades are reflective that most of the staff was not professionally trained till then. Therefore, the provision of accepting the existing staff on six month working experience was accepted. But at the same time it has recommended that in future recruitment, the practice of appointing a person, without the prescribed professional qualifications should be abolished. This was required to make the libraries an intellectual workshop and the heart of Academic Institutions.

In early years, the quantum of work in Academic Libraries has been very less. Services like reference were not in existence even. But now-a-days the situation has altogether different. Libraries are coming up as service centre and working as communication agencies. Most of the University Libraries have been organised on the UGC recommended pattern, comprising number of sections to execute various functions and services which can be groupped as under:

> Book Section, Periodical Section, Documentation Section, Technical Section, Reference Section, Circulation Section, Maintenance Section , Administration Section, Manuscript Section, etc.

According to the needs, university libraries has gone to department and Institute Libraries. These libraries generally work under Central Library for all practical purposes.

The library services now-a-days are of very complex nature. As a result Librarians job today have also become highly complex. The professional skill must be given due importance. Another reason, the

University libraries, are used by the scholars, therefore, the library professionals should also be scholarly to understand the quality of service and scholarly language. The staff therefore, should be extended training facilities or refreshers courses in the subject to update with modern developments. In present context with computer application training and refresher courses have become extremely essential and more relevant. To produce professionally trained staff a good number of university and professional associations should be encouraged to impart various level training courses.

The Review Committee (1981) was of the view that the provision of five per cent of the book grant for additional staff for processing and cataloguing of books is totally inadequate. The Commission, may therefore, consider the need for making specific provision for support towards the appointment of technical staff in the University Libraries. To achieve the standard of teaching and research the role of library services was very much accepted and on the recommendations of committees like Panel of Library and Information Science, Pay Revision Committee and through government orders, the efforts have been made to improve the professional skill. In Eighth Plan guidelines for universities under faculty improvement the provision have been made that the universities may utilise 20 to 25 per cent of the grants for purpose of creating new posts of academic staff, technical staff and supporting professional staff for libraries. As a further step it may also consider to advise universities to use 10 per cent of the library book grants for the purchase of computers and non book material like cassettes etc.

Revision of Pay Scales and Qualifications

To improve the professional quality and quality of library services the UGC recommended revision of scales of pay and qualifications for the various professional library categories such as Librarian, Deputy Librarian, Assistant Librarian and College Librarian.

The gravity of librarians service was well recognised by the Sadhar Commission (1917-1918). And Librarians were accepted as an officers of the university. It recommended the librarian should be appointed by the executive council on the recommendation of the academic council. He should have the salary and status of a university professor, and should be ex-officio member of the academic council. The salary scales of librarians working in the university system were revised vide

UGC letter No. 63-2/60 (SS) dated January 18, 1961. The Commission decided professionally qualified library staff for salary revision purpose should be treated as Academic staff. Junior professional staff in university libraries may be placed on the same scales as lecturers in the college or university and senior professional staff may be placed in Readers or Professors scales according to their qualifications and experience. It was further revised in 1962 and 1968. Government of India, Ministry of Education and Culture vide its letter No. 1-41/74-U.I. dated January 7, 1977 revised the scales effective from January 1, 1973 and after careful consideration further decided to upgrade the scales at par with teachers, effective from 1st April, 1980. Government provisions of 80 per cent financial assistance of the expenditure involved in upgrading was made for States, if they wish to upgrade the scale of pay in State universities and in colleges affiliated to them. The Assistance was extended for the period from April 1, 1980 to March 31, 1985 for post existing as on January 1, 1973 subject to the fulfilment of prescribed qualifications laid down by the UGC. Separate set of qualifications for existing incumbents and for future recruitment of various categories was recommended. While upgrading scales the following points were stressed to improve the quality

(i) Scales will be admissible to those who fulfil prescribed qualifications.
(ii) The Selection should be made by duly constituted Committee of experts.

The Commission (UGC) appointed a committee on December 24, 1983 under the Chairmanship R.C. Mehrotra, to consider the revision of pay scales, career/professional development and Service conditions of teachers in the Universities and Colleges. In Oct., 1985 the Committee was requested to include Librarians also. The Committee submitted its recommendation to the Commission on 3rd Sept., 1986. The main recommendations of the Committee are as follows.

"The principle of parity has been established in the matter of scales of pay between University and College teachers and librarians in the Universities and Colleges. In the case of teachers, the committee has recommended pay scales in the existing framework, the same may be applied to pay scales of these categories. These pay scales may, therefore, be treated as notional and would have to be converted in the light of the recommendations that while converting these scales, it should be ensured that the librarians in Universities and Colleges are not put to any financial disadvantage and envisaged parity is maintained".

The following pay scales were recommended for the various categories of librarians in the universities and colleges by the committee.

Universities	*Payscale in the existing framework (Rs.)*
(i) Assistant University Librarian/ Documentation Officer	700-40-1100-50-1600
(ii) Assistant University Librarian (Senior Scale) Doc. Officer (Senior Scale)	1200-50-1300-60-1900
(iii) Assistant University Librarian (Selection Grade) Doc. Officer (Selection Grade)	2000-125/2 - 2250
(iv) Deputy University Librarian	1500-60-1800-100-2000-125/2 - 2250
(v) University Librarian	1800-100-2000-125/2 2750-125-3000
Colleges	
(i) College Librarian	700-40-1100-50-1600
(ii) College Librarian (Senior Scale)	1200-50-1300-60-1900
(iii) College Librarian (Selection Grade)	2000-125/2 - 2250

The recommendations are accepted by the Government of India and orders are issued to grant revised pay scales and qualifications. The revised pay scales are approved same as for teachers. The revision will be only applicable to those who are receiving 1973 revision at par with teachers. Cases of those Librarians who are in the lower scale have inviting attentation for assessment to grant revision. The revision was effective from Ist January, 1986. Detailed document containing comprehensive information on various service matters is as on Annexure 5.7.

Ministry of Human Resource Development, Deptt. of Education vide its letter No. 1-21/87-U.1 dated 22nd July, 1988 (Annexure 5.7) revised the pay scales of Librarians effective from Ist January, 1986. These orders made provision that "Recruitment of the post of Assistant

Librarian, Deputy Librarian and Librarian in the Universities and Colleges shall be on the basis of merit through all India advertisement and Selection". Promotion to the post of Deputy Librarian and librarian will only be considered for those who fulfil the criteria prescribed. The candidate who fulfil minimum basic qualifications will have to appear to qualify a comprehensive eligibility test conducted by the UGC or its agency.

The persons holding Ph.D. degree or M.Phil. in Library Science at the time of recruitment will be given three or one extra increment, as the case may be in the scale of Rs. 2200–4000 alongwith the benefit of corresponding years service for the purpose of promotion.

In subsequent steps the qualifications were further revised vide letter No. 1-96/81 (CP/MP) dated 31 August, 1984. In supersession to these orders the qualifications were further revised vide letter No. 1-9/89 (CPP-1) dated 20th Feb., 1990.

The grades and qualifications of the main three categories Librarian, Deputy Librarian, Assistant Librarian and College Librarian in their emergence have been brought out on the basis of the official documents. The effort is to depict the professional picture to visualise the quality recognition of services.

A

Order No. 63-2/60 (SS)	*Dated 18th January, 1961*
Professional Senior (Professor)	(a) First or Second class B.A./B.Sc./B.Com. degree plus first or second class M.Lib. Sc. degree (two years course) *OR* First or Second class M.A./M.Sc./ degree and first or second class B.Lib.Sc. or one year diploma course in Library Science. (b) At least 10 years experience as Librarian or working in a responsible professional capacity in a library.

		(c) Recognised research experience of work on special projects.
Order No. 63-2/61 (SS)		*Dated 1st May, 1962*
Professional Senior (Professor)	(Rs. 1100-1500)	Same as above
Order No. 29-20/66 U.1.		*Dated 6th September, 1968*
	(Rs. 1100-1600)	Subject to the fulfilment of conditions of educational qualification and experience
Order No. 50-20/68 (CO)		*Dated 23rd September, 1968*
		(a) First or Second class M.A./-M.Sc./M.Com. plus a first or Second class B.Lib.Sc. or a diploma in Library Science. The degree of M.Lib. Science being a preferential qualification. (b) At least 10 years experience as a Librarian or of work in a responsible professional capacity in a University Library. (c) Good Academic qualifications and research experience with publications. The Selection must be made by a duly constituted committee of experts. The qualifications general must be comparable to those of professor in the Universities.

Order No. F.2-1/82 U.1. *Dated 15th Dec., 1982*

Librarian	(Rs.1500-2500) (Rs. 1500-60-1800-100-2000-125/2-2500)	(a) First or Second Class M.A./M.Sc./M.Com. plus a First or Second Class B.Lib. Science or a diploma in Library Science. The degree of M.Lib.Sc. being a preferential qualification. (b) At least 10 years' experience as Librarian or in a responsible professional capacity in a University Library. (c) Good academic qualification and research experience (with publications). The qualifications must be in general, comparable to those of Professors in the Universities.

Order No. F. 1-96/81 (CP/MP) *Dated 31st August, 1984*

Librarian	(Rs. 1500-60-1800-100-2000-125/2-2500)	(a) First or Second class M.Lib.Sc. or M.A./M.Sc./M.Com. plus a First or Second class B.Lib.Sc. or Diploma in Library Science. (b) At least ten years experience as Librarian or in a responsible professional capacity in a University Library. (c) Ph.D. degree or equivalent research work in the field relevant to the Profession. (d) In certain situation in academic libraries, training in Computerization, Information Technology/Specialised areas may be taken into consideration.

Order No. F. 1-21/87- U.1.		*Dated 22nd July, 1988*
Librarian	(Rs. 4500-150-5700-200-7300)	As above.
Order No. F. 1-9/89 (CCP-1)		*Dated 20th Feb., 1990*
Librarian	(Rs. 4500-150-5700-200-7300)	(i) Master's Degree in Library Science/Information Science Documentation with at least fifty-five per cent marks or its equivalent grade and a consistently good academic record. (ii) One year specialisation in an area of information technology/Archives and Manuscript keeping Master's Degree in an area of thrust in the institution. (iii) At least ten years as a Deputy Librarian in a University Library or fifteen years experience as a College Librarian. (iv) Evidence of innovative library service and Organisation of Published work. *Desirable:* M.Phil/Ph.D. degree in Library Science/Information Science/Documentation/Archives and Manuscript keeping.

B

Order No. 63-2/60 (SS)		*Dated 18th January, 1961*
Professional Senior (Reader)		(a) First or Second class B.A./B.Sc./B.Com. degree plus first or Second class M.Lib.Sc. degree (two years course).

	OR First or Second class M.A./-M.Sc. degree and first and Second class B.Lib.Sc. or one year diploma course in Library Science. (b) Five years experience as Librarian or of working in a responsible professional capacity in a library.
Order No. 63-2/61 (SS)	*Dated 1st May, 1962*
Professional Senior (Rs. 700-1100) (Reader)	Same as above
Order No. 29-20/66 U.1.	*Dated 6th September, 1968*
Professional Senior (Rs. 700-1250) (Reader)	It was recommended for those who were already getting the Scales of the third plan period.
Order No. 50-20/68 (CU)	*Dated 23rd September, 1968*
	(a) First or Second class M.A./-M.Sc./M.Com. plus a first or Second class B.Lib.Sc. or Diploma in Library Science. The degree of M.Lib.Sc. being a preferential qualification. (b) At least 7 years experience as librarian or of work in a responsible professional capacity in a library. (c) Good academic qualifications and research experience with publications. The selection must be made by a duly con-

stituted committee of experts. The qualifications must be in general comparable to those of reader in the Universities.

Order No. 2-1/82 U.1 *Dated 15th Dec., 1982*

Deputy Librarian	(Rs. 1200-50-1300-60-1900)	(a) First or Second Class M.A./M.Sc. M.Com., plus a first or Second class B.Lib.Sc. or Diploma in Library Science. The degree of M.Lib.Sc. being a preferential qualification. (b) At least 7 years experience as Librarian or in a responsible professional capacity in a Library. (c) Good academic qualifications and research experience (with publications). The qualifications must be in general, comparable to those of Readers in the Universities.

Order No. 1-96/81 (CP/MP) *Dated 31st Aug., 1984*

Deputy Librarian	(Rs. 1200-50-1300-60-1900	(a) First or Second Class M.Lib. Sc. or M.A./M.Sc./M.Com. plus a First or Second Class B.Lib.Sc. or Diploma in Library Science. (b) At least seven years experience as Librarian or in a responsible Professional capacity in a University Library. (c) Ph.D. Degree or equivalent research work in the field relevant to the profession.

		(d) In certain situations in academic Libraries, Training in Computerization/Information Technology/ Specialised areas may be taken into consideration.

Order No. 1-21/87 U.1 *Dated 22nd July, 1988*

Deputy Librarian	(Rs. 3700-125-4950-150-5700)	As above

Order No. F -9/89 (CPP-1) *Dated 20th Feb., 1990*

Deputy Librarian	(Rs. 3700-125-4950-150-5700)	(i) Master's Degree in Library Science/Information Science/Documentation with at least fifty-five per cent marks or its equivalent grade and a consistently good academic record; (ii) One year specialisation in an area of information technology/archives and Manuscript keeping or Master's Degree in an area of thrust in the Institution; (iii) Eight years experience as an Assistant University Librarian/College Librarian; and (iv) Evidence of innovative library services, Published work and professional commitment; *Desirable:* M.Phil/Ph.D. Degree in Library Science/Information Science/Documentation/Archives and Manuscript keeping.

C

Order No. 63-2/60 (SS)	*Dated 18th January, 1961*
Professional Junior (Lecturer)	First or Second Class B.A./ B.Sc./B.Com. degree plus first or Second Class M.Lib.-Sc. degree (two years course) *OR* First or Second Class M.A./-M.Sc. degree and first or Second Class B.Lib. Science or one year diploma course in Library Science.
Order No. 63-2/61 (SS)	*Dated 1st May, 1962*
Professional Junior (Rs. 400-800) (Lecturer)	Same as above
Order No. 29-20/66 U.I. Effective from 1.4.1966	*Dated 6th Sept., 1968*
Professional Junior (Rs. 400-950) (Lecturer)	But in the case of professional Junior the qualifications prescribed above must be insisted upon and revised grades may be given to persons who, as and when improve upon their qualifications. Their placement in revised scales must be subject to the screening by a duly constituted committee of experts.
Order No. 50-20/68 (CU)	*Dated 23rd September, 1968*
Assistant Librarian	First or Second Class B.A./B.Sc./B.Com. Degree plus a first or Second Class

		M.Lib. Degree *OR* First or Second Class M.A./M.Sc./M.Com. Degree and a First or Second Class B.Lib.Sc. or a Diploma in Library Science.
Order No. 63-2/61 (SS)		*Dated 1st May, 1962*
College Librarians		College Librarians who possess the qualifications indicated in respect of Professional Junior may be placed on the same scale of pay as Lecturers in the college.
Order No. 29-20/66 U.I.		*Dated 6th September, 1968*
Professional Junior (Lecturer)	(Rs. 300-600)	(a) M.A./M.Sc./M.Com. Degree and a Diploma in Library Science. (b) For existing B.A./B.Sc./-B.Com. degree with a Diploma in Library Science or B.Lib.Sc. ordinarily at least five years experience as Librarian. (c) The qualification must be insisted upon (d) Placement to revised scale must be by a duly constituted Committee of experts.
Order No. 2-1/82 U.I.		*Dated 15th Dec., 1982*
Assistant Librarian/ Documentation Officer/College Librarian	(Rs. 700-1600) (Rs. 700-40-1100-50-1600)	(a) First or Second Class B.A./ B.Sc./B.Com. degree plus a first or Second Class M.Lib. Sc. Degree. *OR*

		First or Second Class M.A./M.Sc./M.Com. Degree and a first or Second Class B.Lib.Sc. or a Diploma in Library Science.

Order No. 2-1/82 U.I — *Dated 15th December, 1982*

Assistant Librarian	(Rs. 700-1600)	(a) Good academic record with at least a High Second Class Master's Degree in a subject other than Library Science. (b) Master's Degree in Library Science with first or High Second Class.

Order No. F. 1-96/81 (CP/MP) — *Dated 31st August, 1984*

Assistant Librarian	(Rs. 700-40-1100-50-1600)	(a) Good academic record with at least a high second class Master's degree in a subject other than Library Science. (b) Master's degree in Library Science with First Class or High Second Class. The qualifications were relaxed with 10 years experience vide D. No. F. 22-5/05 (AE) dated April 15, 1925

Order No. 1-21/87 U.I. — *Dated 22nd July, 1988*

Assistant Librarian	(2200-75-2800-100-4000)
Senior Scale	(3000-100-3500-125-5000)
Selection grade	(3700-125-4950-150-5700)

Order No. 2-1/82 U.I.		*Dated 15th Dec., 1982*
College Librarian	(Rs. 700-40-1100-50-1300-Assessment-50-1600)	(a) Good Academic record with at least a High Second Class Master's Degree in a Subject other than Library Science. (b) Master's Degree in Library Science with First Class or High Second Class.
Order No. F1-96/81 (CP/MP)		*Dated 31st August, 1984*
		As above
Order No. 2-3 84 U.I.		*Dated 6th Jan., 1987*
		Existing incumbents in colleges who were appointed on or before 31.12.72 were allowed scale 700-1600 with relaxation of qualification i.e. without insisting on a first or second class in the degree, diploma or other prescribed qualifications. This relaxation of qualification was also extended to central universities vide letter No. 4-1(1)/87 (CR/ER) dated April, 1987.
Order No. F 1-96/81 (EP/MP)		*Dated 31st August, 1984*
		As above
Order No. 1-21/87 U.I.		*Dated 22nd July, 1988*
		The 700-1600 scale was revised to 2200-75-2800-100-400. Senior scale 3000-

		100-3500-125-5000. Selection grade 3700-125-4950-150-5700.

Order No. F 1-9/89 (CPP-I) *Dated 20th Feb., 1990*

Assistant University Librarian/College Librarian/Documentation Officer:	(Rs. 2200-75-2800-100-4000)	(i) Qualifying the National level test conducted for the purpose by the UGC or any other agency approved by the UGC. (ii) Master' Degree in Library Science/Information Science/Documentation or an equivalent professional degree with atleast fifty-five per cent marks or its equivalent grade plus a consistently good academic record; *OR* Master's Degree in Arts/Science/Commerce or equivalent degree with at least fifty five per cent marks or its equivalent grade with Bachelor's Degree in Library Science/Information Science/Documentation or an equivalent professional degree with atleast fifty-five per cent marks or its equivalent grade plus a consistently good academic record.

The Commission is in practice of reviewing the Staff position of the libraries of constituent Colleges of the Delhi University. The orders 1-18/63 (CUP) dated 25th Sept., 1964 on the Review Committee recommendations laid down the following strength of staff.

A. *For Day Classes*

1. Librarian	In the pay scale 400-800 subject to the incumbent having qualifications prescribed by the U.G.C.
2. Assistant Librarian	One in the pay Scale of Rs. 130-280 and on one in the pay scale of Rs. 110-180
3. Typist	
4. Library Attendant	

(a) *For a library working for normal hours*

No. of Books	*Library Attendants*
Up to 15,000	2
More than 15,000 but less than 30,000	3
30,000 and above	4

(b) *For a library working 12 hours a day*

No. of Books	*Library Attendant*
Up to 15,000	4
More than 15,000 and less than 30,000	6
30,000 and above	6

B. *For Evening Classes*

Librarian	In the scale Rs. 400-800 subject to qualifications prescribed by the U.G.C.
Library Assistant	One in the pay scale of Rs. 130-280
Typist	One in the pay scale Rs. 110-180.
Library Attendants	As in the case of College libraries working for normal duration of the College.

UGC vide letter No. 1-35/67 (CU) dated 18th Feb., 1968 approved the creation of additional post of Professional Assistant in the Scale of Rs. 250-400 in the Libraries of Constituent Colleges of the Delhi University.

The UGC vide its letter No. 47-33/67 (CU) dated 15th Feb., 1968 revised the Scales of pay of Library Attendants as under:

Library Attendant	Existing	Revised
	75-95	80-110
Sr. Lib. Attendant		95-115
Sr. Lib. Attendant	Matriculation or its equivalent with good handwriting and previous experience of library work.	
Jr. Lib. Attendant	Essential – Matriculation Desirable-Experience of having worked in some Library.	

Further revised vide letter No. 47-33/67 (CU) Dated 3rd July, 1968
In the scale Rs. 80-110

Order No. 63-2/61 (SS) *Dated 19th May, 1965*

Professional Junior — May be placed in the Scale of Pay Rs. 250-400 prescribed for Professional Assistants.

Career Advancement

"Every Assistant Librarian in a University and a Librarian in a College, who is in the Scale of pay Rs. 2200-4000 will be placed in a Senior Scale of Rs. 3000-5000 if he/she has

(a) Completed 8 years services after regular appointment, with relaxation as provided in para 7 of this Circular No.
(b) Participated in two refresher courses summer institutes, each of approximately four weeks, duration or engaged in other appropriate continuing education programme of comparable quality as may be specified by the UGC, and
(c) Constant by Satisfactory performance appraisal reports.

22-4/85 (AE) 15th March, 1985

To rationalise the scales of pay of Professional Assistants in central universities, pay scale of 550-900 fulfilling the qualifications prescribed for the post of Assistant Librarian of pay scale of 700-1600 may be placed in the scale of pay 700-1600 with effect from Ist April, 1985. The persons who does fulfil qualifications there case was taken separately.

The cadre of Professional Assistant was studied by Cadre Review Committee for Central Universities of UGC and the scales were further revised as 2200-4000 for those who were in the scale of pay of Rs. 700-1600.

All existing incumbents of these posts in the Universities and Colleges, who are in the Scale of pay of Rs. 700-1600 and who have completed 3 years of service on 1.1.1986 will be placed through a process of screening/selection in the Scale of Rs. 3000-5000. The benefit of service will be provided as per the provision available for the initial placement.

Every Assistant Librarian in the Universities, who has been placed in the Senior Scale will be eligible for promotion to the post of Deputy Librarian in the Scale of pay of Rs. 3700-5700 if he/she has:

(a) Completed 3 years of service in the Senior Scale provided that the requirement of 8 years will be relaxed if his/her total service is not less than 16 years.
(b) Obtained a Ph.D. degree or an equivalent published work.
(c) Made significant contributions to the development of library service in the University as evidenced by self-assessment, reports of references, professional improvement in the library service etc.
(d) Participated in two refresher courses, summer Institute each of approximately 4 weeks duration or engaged in other appropriate continuing education programmes of comparable quality as may be specified by UGC, after placement in the Senior Scale, and
(e) Constituent by good performance appraised reports.

Promotion to the post of Deputy Librarian will be through a process of selection by a selection committee CDS in the case of promotion to the post of Readers. Post of Deputy Librarian will be created for this purpose by upgrading the post of Assistant Librarian (Senior Scale).

The Assistant Librarians in the Universities in the Senior Scale who do not have Ph.D. degree or equivalent published work, but fulfils the other criteria mentioned in para nine will be placed in the grade of Rs. 3700-5700 subject to the recommendations of the Committee mentioned in para 10 of the orders. They will be designated as

Assistant Librarian in the Selection Grade.

The College Librarians in Colleges, who have been placed in the senior scale will also be eligible for placement in the selection grade for Rs. 3700-5700 if they fulfil the criteria prescribed in the aforesaid orders.

Selection Procedure

The Government has issued orders that the selection for the post of University Librarian, Deputy Librarian, Assistant Librarian, College Librarian and Documentation Officers should be made strictly on merit on an all India basis. The Selection Committee should include two experts not connected with the University. Promotion of candidate to the senior scale and selection grade should also be done on the recommendations of a Selection Committee having atleast one expert not connected with the University.

The Committee on revision of pay scales of librarians and directors of physical education in universities and colleges in its report chapter 3 as on Annexure 5.6 has made various recommendations to improve the quality of university and college library services. It has emphasised the importance, need, role and responsibility of the librarian towards library services.

Norms for Staffing Pattern

The Commission set up an ad-hoc committee to work out norms for staff in University Libraries (1984) under the Chairmanship of Shri Girja Kumar, Librarian, JNU, New Delhi. The Committee analysed the various jobs undertaken by the libraries and submitted its report on norms and standards for staffing pattern in University and College Libraries to the Commission.

Further in 1986 under the chairmanship of Professor G. Padmanabhan, the expert committee on the minimum qualifications, workload etc., for Librarians and Directors of Physical Education was constituted by UGC, which submitted its report on July 9, 1987 as on Annexure 5.1, the Government orders on staff formula are still awaited. Thus the staff formula in practice is known as Ranganathan staff formula (1965) which is skeleton and have become obsolete in changed service conditions. A new staff formula is the need of the age. A partial work on the subject is also developed by the Cadre Review

Committee on Central Universities. The findings of this committee are yet to be cleared by the UGC and the Government.

The norms and standards of library services should also be evolved keeping in view the application of new technologies. Existing conditions should be analysed, examined and different variables such as stock, annual additions, circulation, membership, service, objectives, opening hours should be given due waitage. The exercise will help in knowing what type of man-power is available and what has to be developed to modernise the services. This is also needed to develop a well-equipped and well-managed academic library to the foundation of modern educational structure. As the academic pursuit and library service are basis of development programmes.

As usual it was also first realised by Dr. S.R. Ranganathan who gave a staff formula in the recommendations of 1965 report submitted to UGS under his chairmanship.

The library staff works behind the scene for various operations at the same time it works directly for dissemination of information through circulation and reference desk. New technologies has opened new doors to meet the challenges of the age. Therefore, for determining staff requirement and staff quality there should be evolved formula which should have basis of the job analysis. National body like UGC should work in this direction. Standing Committee for the development of University and College library should be formulated. Inspite of all efforts with haphazard growth and with increasing user population and knowledge explosion the libraries are understaff. Some of the reasons for it may be the following:

(i) Unplanned growth of collections,
(ii) Non availability of any staff formula,
(iii) Job recognition,
(iv) Lack of library culture,
(v) Inadequate funds,
(vi) Poor professional training courses,
(vii) Insufficient technical experts,
(viii) Implementation of policies by non library professionals for recruiting library professional scientific staff, and
(ix) Defective recruitment policies.

Orientation Courses

Review Committee on Library Science (1965) was appointed by the

UGC under the Chairmanship Dr. S.R. Ranganathan to review the standards of teaching and research in Library Sciences in Indian Universities. The introduction of the report gives the picture of the library science training imparted in Indian universities. The library consciousness in our country is a recent development. The university libraries has only expanded or developed library services, mainly though UGC efforts. For maintaining standards of service professional training in librarianship has been realised very much.

It's an established fact that in modern times the function of a librarian is not limited to collect books and lookafter their safety. In the library a scholar or a qualified technical professional has to perform his duties in an intelligent manner to inspire the library users. He has to create ,a real interest and curiosity in the eaders for acquiring knowledge/information, which will in turn cultivate reading habit. Further more in recent past non book developments has made the job of the Librarian/Information scientists more complex.

"Education for libraries began in India in the second decade of the present century with the starting of a library school in the Baroda state in 1911. This was the result of the interest taken by Sayaji Rao Gaekwar, who, impressed by the splendid work done by public libraries in the west, secured the services of an American Librarian Mr. W.C. Bordon as Director of the State Library department. In this chain Mr. Dickensen Librarian, Punjab University, Library started a library school in 1915 which continued till 1946.

Then in 1929 Madras Library Association in collaboration with Madras University started school of library science. The Bengal Library Association initiated in 1935. Similarly, Banaras Hindu University started a Post-graduate Diploma course in 1941. In 1944, University of Bombay and Calcutta University in 1946. In 1946 Delhi University established a Department of Library Science and in 1951, Aligarh Muslim University started a training course and till then number of Universities opening the department in the subject Library and Information Science and at present about eighty-one universities have facility of library sciences education. Some of the institutions are extending correspondence education, vocational courses, evening courses and exclusive courses for women etc.

Training Programme

In 1981, on the recommendations of the sub-committee on

Development of University and College Libraries the Universities were requested to organise training programmes both short-term and long-term for College Librarians. The Sub-committee recommended following Centres to organise such winter/summer courses for College Librarians.

Name of the Centre	*Area to be Covered*
Delhi University	U.P. and M.P.
Punjab University	Punjab, Haryana, HP, J&K, Rajasthan and Union Territory Chandigarh
Bombay	Maharashtra, Gujarat, Goa
Kerala	Kerala, Tamil Nadu and Orissa
Indian Institute of Science, Bangalore	Karnataka, A.P.
Gauhati	W.B., Assam, Bihar, Meghalaya, Manipur, Arunachal Pradesh, Nagaland, Mizoram and Tripura.

Such winter Institutes were organised by the Delhi University and Punjab University during the year 1981-82.

An implementation programme of NEP (1986) and Programme of Action (POA) the commission initiated a scheme to set up Academic Staff College (ASC) with the following functions for the orientation of newly appointed University and college teachers.

Functions of an Academic Staff College

The functions of an Academic Staff College will be to plan, organize, implement, monitor and evaluate orientation courses for newly appointed college/university lecturers within the jurisdiction of one or more universities in a State. An ASC will also organize Refresher courses for serving teachers, and orientation programmes for senior administrators and heads of departments, principals, etc. In the philosophy or orientation and changed management system. specifically an Academic Staff College will:

(a) Formulate a programme of orientation along the broad guidelines.
(b) Identify resource persons in the various fields of specialization needed for running the orientation course, and familiarize such resource persons with the philosophy and guidelines for the orientation Programme.
(c) Set up a documentation centre-cum-library for reference and source materials necessary for orientation courses.
(d) Produce specially designed materials required for effective implementation of the orientation courses.
(e) Monitor the various components and stages of the orientation courses.
(f) Evaluate the effectiveness of the orientation courses.
(g) Organize Refresher Courses for serving teachers.
(h) Organize orientation programmes for Heads of Departments, Principals, Deans of other decision-makers to familiarize them with the philosophy of orientation, in order to enable these senior educational administrators to understand their new roles as supervisors, and to facilitate the reform in higher education through appropriate modification of the management systems at various levels.

As on Annexure 5.2 48 Universities have been identified to run orientation programmes. The detailed schedule of programmes for courses was appeared in University News, April 30, 1990 issue at page 26 to 32.

To discharge the functions of co-ordination and maintenance of standards in teaching and research the statutory responsibilities of the University Grants Commission under UGC Act, 1956, the orientation programmes are being conducted. The main objective of the programme is to enhance the motivation of teachers, ensure systematic orientation in specific subjects, techniques and mythologies and to provides opportunities for professional and career development so that professionals or teachers can fulfil their role and responsibility.

Each ASC is expected to organise eight programmes in a year of four weeks duration each. For such courses 85 to 90 per cent candidate may be from the catchment area and rest can be invited from the outside the state on all India basis.

The scheme of orientation programmes for newly appointed teachers was initiated by the Commission during 1987-88. The scheme covers the library science teachers and working librarians for refresher course purpose. So for following four Staff Colleges are identified to conduct refresher courses in the field of Library Science during 1990-91.

1. S.N.D.T. Women's University	West
2. Osmania University	South
3. A.M.U. Aligarh University	North/Central
4. N.E.H.U.	East
5. Gujarat Vidyapeeth (1900-)	

The following schedule of programmes of refresher courses in library science was announced for the period 1990-91.

Library Science	Osmania University Hyderabad	04.04.90 to 28.04.90 02.05.90 to 26.05.90 03.09.90 to 26.09.90 South 04.02.91 to 28.02.91
-do-	A.M. University Aligarh	23.07.90 to 24.08.90 12.11.90 to 08.12.90 North/Central 11.03.91 to 05.04.91 Central
	N.E.H. University Shillong	10.10.90 to 31.10.90 East
-do-	S.N.D.T. Women's University Bombay.	04.06.90 to 30.06.90 29.10.90 to 29.11.90 West 07.01.91 to 02.02.90

(*Source*: University News)

Refresher Courses

In August, 1988 the UGC identified 93 University department/ Institutions to organise such courses. In the beginning these were for lecturers and later also extended for the working librarians. The duration of courses is three to four weeks. The centre is suppose to organise five refresher courses in the given discipline, up to 31.3.1989 under this programme 4411 newly recruited teachers and 953 in service teachers have participated in the orientation and refresher courses. This member includes the library Science teachers, librarians, and teachers of others disciplines.

The professional refresher courses, Summer Courses are essential to improve efficiency. The courses will improve out book with technical know how and subject innovations. The Commission is providing 100 per cent assistance to the Programme.

Review of University Libraries : University of Delhi

Survey of the University of Delhi Library, Carl M.White (1965) document produced "to dig out relevant information about the university's library problems and report it in a form suitable for fruitful consideration by the authorities who are responsible for the future of the university". The propose of the report was to view the library in its setting, to assess the effectiveness with which its responsibilities are being met, to suggest measures for improvement, and to identify problems, especially problems of longer range, which require further study. The summary recommendations of the committee are as on Annexure 5.5.

The UGC in pursuance of its decision taken on Dec. 4, 1984 appointed committees on January 17, 1986 to review the working of the university of Hyderabad NEHU and JNU. The committee reviewed Hyderabad university library and recommended as on Annexure 5.6.

National Level Test

The Important measure taken by the Commission (UGC) to improve the Standard of research and higher education was introduction of a National Level Test from 1984. This is to award research fellowships as well as to scanning for recruiting professionals. The central aim of this test is to overcome the problems of comparability for bringing uniformity in standards of evaluation in different universities and to ensure that only the best deserving students are selected for the award of fellowship. The test is being conducted for library and Information Science to achieve the objectives. The syllabi in Library Science has been designed as on Annexure 5.3. The Government has also given direction while revising the pay scales to conduct National Level Test for future recruitment of librarians.

Resource Sharing

The Library co-operation, resource sharing or co-ordination is seems very essential keeping in view immense expansion and all round growth in Institutions, students, subjects, research activities and other educational activities. On the other hand the non-book machine readable form of information collections is taking place in the University libraries with a great speed. The ultimate requirement of resource sharing is to broden the resources of library system at the least cost. The machine readable form of information will made possible access to the special collections of Academic and Research libraries. This was the reason the Commission (UGC) has given timely thought and formulated Committee to work for UNILIBNET and later renamed INFLIBNET. The composition of the committee was consisting senior Library Professionals, Scientists, Technologists of various organisations. The Committee has made a comprehensive study of the present scenarium and suggested future programme in the light of emerging technology such as computers and CO-ROM products etc.

"INFLIBNET" will be a computer-communication Network of Libraries and bibliographical information centres. It is a major National effort to improve capability in information transfer and an access, to provide support to Scholarship learning, research and academic pursuits. The participants will be the institutions of higher learning covering all disciplines, R&D Institutions and National Organisations.

It will be major programme towards modernisation of Libraries and Information Centres in the country, with application of computer and communication technologies. Thus INFLIBNET is a multiple function/Service Network. It will offer catalogue based services, data base services, document supply services, collection development and communication based Services, there will be a National Centre for managing, overseating and co-ordination the affairs of the Network and for regional centres which will maintain union catalogue of holdings of Libraries in the regions and database of projects, institutions and specialists. As many as 100 Universities and R&D Institutional libraries will be designated and equipped to serve as Document Resource Centres for purpose of Document Delivery Service. The programme will be in number of phases. The observations and objectives of the programme are as an Annexure 5.4. A centre has been established at Ahmedabad to start with.

As usual the UGC has taken lead by talking on 'INFLIBNET' and 'Mass media education' by welcoming scientific and technological innovations. The idea is floated through Eighth plan gaudelines and proposals have been invited to extand assistance to create infrastructure, equipment and to initiate programmes to improve professional quality.

Suggestions

- There should be a national policy for integrated development of the university and college libraries.
- The objectives of the library development should be defined and the services should be compatible to the requirements.
- The existing infrastructure should be suitably renovated to accommodate innovations and modern technologies.
- The modern equipment should be on National and International standards. The specification for computer and non book collections should be decided by the UGC or some other National body.
- The national pattern of information networking should be adopted to facilitate resource sharing.
- The planning of library development as one unit should be centralised.
- New university and college only be recognised when these have adequate library facilities or services.
- There should be a standing committee of the UGC on university and college libraries development which may review the services and impact of UGC assistance for future plan of action.
- Library assistance should have basis of national policy.
- The faculty and departmental libraries should develop to facilitate researches.
- There should be standing visiting committee comprising library professional to ascertain future development programme.
- The purchase of costly foreign and Indian publications may be controlled by some central agency.
- The planners of university and colleges should be educated or provided initial plan to begin with.
- The development plans can be divided in number of phases.
- New development such as distance educations, adult education,

media education, and women education should be taken care of.

- There should be a review committee after every five years for each library.
- A list compiled by central body for standard references should be recommended to all the university and college libraries.
- Co-operative depositories should be developed to shift less important documents.
- To arrange effective services a continuous and systematic approach to know the needs of users of education system as well as library service centres is required.
- There is a absolute urgency to make substantially higher allocations to welcome application of modern equipment such as computer, Disks etc.
- The library services should be improved or standardised both qualitatively and quantitatively. The quality of service should be research oriented suited to the academic, research and teaching programmes of the universities. The services should meet especialised requirements of the modern age.
- Mass media should be used for promoting library culture.
- There should be social motivation that on every occasion the books should be gifted as social interaction. On National celebrations we should also distribute books on teachings or on, moral values etc.
- User education should be the part of the curricula and media slogan as well.
- The university libraries should initiate for especialised services such as SDI, user profile, computer database etc.
- Efforts should be made to invent techniques to generate information products and services.
- Efforts should be made to create expertise for using the information flow. New knowledge can be developed by generating the available information.
- The existing professional strength should be recharged with developments of profession. For this the short term programmes or training can do.
- The library services should be under a system like other cadres so that every professional should have promotional channel of service.
- Carrier development opportunities as created for teaching staff should also be extended to library professionals.
- Library should be recognised as teaching institution not a non-

- Library should be recognised as teaching institution not a non-teaching operation as recognised in present by some of the states.
- To improve the quality of service parametres of expansion has to be laid down.
- Vocational/summer/winter courses should be arranged for inservice professionals.
- Central assistance should be provided to do research in library and information service.
- The immediate steps should be taken to bring out overall improvement in building, equipment, collections and professional staff to achieve co-operation and modernised effective services.
- Regional library centres or regional libraries depositeries should be encouraged to have comprehensive collections and the subjects identified.
- The service can also be pooled by creating UGC regional service centres to facilitate users.
- While considering for grants, the location of library, year of establishment and enrolment should be taken care of.
- Union list of periodicals subscribed by a identified Zone should be prepared and circulated to reduce duplicate purchase.

Cultural Exchange Programme

The Commission (UGC) implements such of the cultural exchange agreements entered into the Government of India with foreign government as are assigned to it, these programmes involve exchange of library scientists and professional also for lecture cum study, exchange of views, scholarships and fellowships, development of bilateral academic links, organisation of joint seminars and training, etc. Those programme are helpful in improving the quality of service. The grants are allocated to universities under the head 'unassigned Grants'.

Seminars, Summer Institute and Workshops

The Commission has been supporting the efforts of universities and colleges in providing opportunities for teachers and research workers to keep abreast of modern development in their fields of study with provision of grants towards organisation of Seminars, Symposia, refresher courses, workshops, conference etc. This is an important programme under faculty improvement activities". The provisions are made to meet to and fro expenses of the scholar who receives

ANNEXURES

ANNEXURE 1.1

The UGC Powers and Functions

As per UGC Act 1956, the Commission may:

(a) Enquire into the financial needs of universities;

(b) allocate and disburse, out of the funds of the Commission, grants to Universities established or incorporated by or under a Central Act for the maintenance and development of such Universities or for any other general or specified purpose;

(c) allocate and disburse, out of the fund of the Commission, such grants to other universities as it may deem (necessary or appropriate for the development of such Universities or for the development of such Universities or for the maintenance, or development or both, of any specified activities of such universities) or for any other general or specified purpose:

Provided that in making any grants to any such university, the Commission shall give consideration to the development of the University concerned, its financial needs, the standard attained by it and the national purposes which it may serve;

(cc) allocate and disburse out of the fund of the Commission, such grants to institutions deemed to be universities in pursuance of a declaration made by the Central Government under Section 3, as it may deem necessary, for one or more of the following purposes namely:

(i) for maintenance in special cases,
(ii) for development, and
(iii) for any other general or specified purpose.

(ccc) establish, in accordance with the regulations made under this

Act, institutions for providing common facilities, services and programmes for a group of universities or for the universities in general and maintain such institutions or provide for their maintenance by allocating and disbursing out of the fund of the Commission such grants as the Commission may deem necessary;

(d) recommend to any university the measures necessary for the improvement of university education and advise the university upon the action to be taken for the purpose of implementing such recommendations;

(e) advise the Central Government or any State Government on the allocation of any grants to universities for any general or specified purpose out of the Consolidated Fund of India or the Consolidated Fund of the State, as the case may be;

(f) advise any authority, if such advice is asked for, on the establishment of a new university or on proposals connected with the expansion of the activities of any University;

(g) advise the Central Government or any State Government or University on any question which may be referred to the Commission by the Central Government or the State Government or the University, as the case may be;

(h) collect information on all such matters relating to university education in India and other countries as it thinks fit and make the same available to any university;

(i) require a university to furnish it with such information as may be needed relating to the financial position of the University or the studies in the various branches of learning undertaken in that university, together with all the rules and regulation in that university relating to the standard of teaching and examination in the university respecting each of such branches of learning;

(j) perform such other functions as may be prescribed or as may be deemed necessary by the Commission for advancing the cause of higher education in India or as may be incidental or conducive to the discharge of the above functions".

ANNEXURE 1.2

INFLIBNET Programme Recommendations

1. INFLIBNET may be established as a nationally important mission to provide library and bibliographic information support to academic and research communities in the country.
2. INFLIBNET may be implemented as a Eighth Five Year (1990–95) Plan Project in two phases of two years duration each.
3. INFLIBNET may be managed as one of the Technology Missions. Alternatively, it could be a registered society with a Council and a Governing Body. It is to function as an independent organisation, after initiation by the UGC.
4. INFLIBNET will encompass institutions of higher learning, R&D institutions, ICAR, ICMR, ICSSR, ICSR, ICHR, CSO, Indira Gandhi National Centre for Arts and such others engaged in academic and research pursuits.
5. The Government of India should finance the project in full.
6. Possibility of seeking external assistance under UN and bilateral programmes for setting up the Communication System and for other hardware equipment may be explored.
7. The UGC may be entrusted with the responsibility of carrying out pre-project activities and overseeing the implementation in the initial stages.
8. Participation in the network may be made as voluntary, by means of institutional agreement. However, the participating libraries are required to fulfil the objectives, functions and services of the INFLIBNET.
9. Adoption of uniform standards throughout the network in matters of techniques, procedures and methods is an important requirement on the part of participating libraries and it must be made as an obligatory requirement.
10. Network participants will use common/compatible software and hardware for the computerisation programme.
11. A suitable organisation may be entrusted with the task of developing application software packages for library automation

and information retrieval.

12. By associating organisations having expertise and experience, the UGC may take steps in the initial stages to design the architecture, develop necessary technology and set up the Communication System of INFLIBNET.
13. The Communication System may be a hybrid version of satellite and terrestrial networking. Distant places will be inter-connected via satellite links. Nodes in a city, when they are many, will be inter-connected by Local Area Network.
14. The Communication System will have a Central Hub and 400 Ground Terminals at 150 university libraries, 50 PG Centres/autonomous colleges and 200 others, comprising R&D institutions, Document Resource Centres and Sectoral Information Centres.
15. A National Centre and four Regional Centres may be created newly within the framework of INFLIBNET.
16. 170 university libraries and 500 colleges are to be supported for library automation programme.
17. 100 libraries having rich collection, are to be identified and supported for undertaking document delivery service and they will be designated as Document Resource Centres.
18. The UGC Information Centres, the present and proposed, NISSAT Sectoral Centres and other information centres which perform national level functions may be brought within the fold of the INFLIBNET for database services in specialised subject fields.
19 Retrospective conversion of catalogue data, being a massive operation, should be carried out as a crash programme, in a time bound manner during Ist Phase of the Project (1990–92) at the National Centre/Regional Centre by employing a special team for the purpose.
20. Personnel, in appropriate quality and in adequate quantity, should be provided for at the various levels/nodes of the INFLIBNET.
21. Training of personnel, for present and future requirements, in aspects such as computerisation, communication use, data preparation, online search, etc. should be provided for.

ANNEXURE 2.1

Summary of Chief Recommendations made by the Committee for the Development of College and University Libraries (1965)

UGC Grants

A period of 17 months should be allowed for the proper Utilisation of the UGC grant for reading and kindred materials, to facilitate book-selection and book-purchase along useful and economic lines without disturbing the weekly rhythm of the administration work of the library and the normal reference and circulation service to readers.

A library may be allowed to spend up to 1/5th of the Commission's grant for reading and kindred materials on the staff required to select and complete the purchases of the materials and to complete the technical work and the processing necessary to bring them into active use.

Commission's grant to a university library should be determined according to an agreed per capita formula.

Subject to local variation, the capacity of the university to spend, and the amount at the disposal of the Commission, for grant for reading and kindred materials, Rs. 15 per capita on the basis of students registered in the university and Rs. 200 per teacher may be given as grant to a university library for the time being. These figures should be revised periodically in the light of the changes in the cost of books and periodicals.

In the case of an affiliating university the number of students and teachers to be counted should be determined in the light of local conditions.

In the case of a newly started university which is not more than five years old, an additional grant up to a sum of Rs. 300,000 may be given the build up the initial stock of reading materials, such as periodicals, Publications, reference books, and advanced treatises.

These universities may be given permission to spend this amount within a period of 3 years.

Whenever schemes for the development of Postgraduate Departments are accepted by the Commission, some assistance should be given for the purchase of reading and kindred materials and bringing them into active use.

The entire library finance of a university or a college library should provided by the Commission and the State Government.

The Commission and the State Government should decide from time to time the proportion in which their respective grants to a university or a college library should be determined.

The Commission and the State Government should have an agreed understanding between them that each will actually pay its own share of the library grant.

The Commission should not ordinarily withdraw or lower its grant to a university or a college library because the State Government fails to provide the corresponding matching grant.

The library grant in any year should be based on the statistical data of the preceding year.

Sources for Library Finance

Between the Commission and the State Government it must be decided in what proportion 'he library finance should be shared. This proportion will depend among other factors on the taxing powers of the Union Government and the State Government. Perhaps the State Government may pay one-fifth of the requirements of a university or a college library and the Commission the remaining four-fifths, for the time being. The capital expenditure of a university or a college library also will have to be provided similarly. However, if the Commission would pay its share of the grant only on condition that the State Government pays its own share or vice-versa, it would nullify the educational purpose based on a realistic scale of social values and the very intention of the Commission in providing each university and college library with adequate finance to serve the students, teachers, and research follows with all the necessary literature. Such an inter-dependence should be avoided.

The university and the college authorities should find it possible to see that the facility mentioned in section 41 of the report is not abused and is not taken by the university or the college library as a licence to be slack in the appropriation of the book-fund according to the weekly rhythm described in section III of chapter 8 of the report.

Library Fund

The library fund of a university or a college should be maintained and operated as a separate library account.

To make the spending of book-fund useful and to avoid its being dissipated on the rush-purchase of any materials readily available in the nearby market, the unappropriated amount of the budget should not be lost to the library, but should be carried forward to the credit of the library and be available for inclusion in the budget of the next year, as an addition to the normal allotment. Our chief book market is now thousands of miles away. Scholarly treatises, research materials, and particularly back volumes of learned periodicals take a long time in searching and procuring. Therefore, this provision for the revival of unspent balance in the next year's budget is quite essential.

Each library should:

1. Spread the utilisation of the grant received from the Commission for reading and kindred materials as uniformly as possible over the entire period of 17 months allowed for purchase;
2. Avoid hastening to spend the grant somehow on the purchase of whatever is available for immediate delivery without fully satisfying itself, about the actual or anticipated demand of the reading materials purchased;
3. Complete all the administrative and technical work on the reading materials and release them for use by readers as expeditiously as possible, say, within less than one month of their receipt in the library;
4. Allocate the total book-fund equitably over all the disciplines pursued by the parent body, subject to the availability of worthwhile reading and kindred materials in the different disciplines and the special extraordinary needs, if any, of particular disciplines;
5. Avoid duplication of learned periodicals and reference books;
6. Minimise duplication of advanced treatises;
7. Purchase a reasonable number of copies of books of the text book standard; and
8. Distribute the share of the total book-fund of each discipline, equitably on current learned periodicals, their back-volumes, reference books, advanced treatises, and text-books.

It is desirable and economical for the selection of current learned periodicals and their back volumes to be coordinated among the libraries of a locality or a region, so as to minimise duplication and maximise the number of distinct periodicals available in the region, in order that the book-fund of each institution may go the longest way.

Without prejudice to the recurring local needs of students and research workers in different subjects, the libraries of a locality or a region should by mutual agreement specialise in stated subjects and make their collection in them as complete as possible for the requirements of research and invoke the aid of inter-library loan for books in frequent demand in subjects in which they do not specialise.

To prevent any prejudice to the readers' requirements being caused by the co-ordination of selection and purchase mentioned in Secs. 24 and 25, the libraries should co-operate with one another in inter-library loan and, whenever warranted, in exchange of reading materials, so that they are housed where they are in greatest demand.

The Commission may frame a set of Rules for Inter-Library Loan and commend them to the University Libraries.

To facilitate inter-library loan and co-ordination of selection, the UGC should promote the production and maintenance of a union catalogue of the learned periodicals and the book in foreign languages other than English and rare books necessary for research in the humanities and the social science along the lines in which the INSDOC is doing for the natural sciences.

ANNEXURE 3.1

UGC Grants to the Universities for Library Buildings till 31st March, 1973

Sl. No.	University	Approved Cost	UGC Share	Grants Paid
1	2	3	4	5
1.	Agra	29,575.00	19,716.00	9,000.00
2.	Aligarh	18,30,959.00	18,30,959.00	18,10,430.00
3.	Allahabad	16,91,400.00	14,60,933.00	13,22,667.00
4.	Andhra	11,14,000.00	7,42,666.00	6,05,000.00
5.	Annamalai	9,00,000.00	6,00,000.00	5,14,678.00
6.	BHU	8,29,520.00	8,29,520.00	8,37,373.00
7.	Bangalore	10,00,000.00	6,66,000.00	2,50,000.00
8.	Baroda	15,01,745.00	7,67,780.00	6,67,447.00
9.	Bhagalpur	10,00,000.00	6,66,667.00	9,46,000.00
10.	Bihar	6,60,147.00	4,00,000.00	5,85,000.00
11.	Bombay	6,22,000.00	4,14,667.00	4,14,666.00
12.	Burdwan	10,00,000.00	6,66,666.00	6,61,000.00
13.	Calcutta	34,35,960.00	22,90,639.00	19,10,000.00
14.	Calicut	—	—	1,18,500.00
15.	Delhi	17,83,000.00	17,83,00.00	12,70,000.00
16.	Dibrugarh	6,00,000.00	4,00,000.00	—
17.	Gauhati	12,48,000.00	8,32,000.00	8,02,906.00
18.	Gorakhpur	14,59,966.00	9,41,242.00	9,50,200.00
19.	Gujarat	9,21,674.00	5,33,333.00	5,80,000.00
20.	Indore	16,51,750.00	10,00,000.00	6,60,000.00
21.	Jabalpur	9,98,803.00	6,65,869.00	5,95,000.00
22.	Jadavpur	7,81,594.00	5,21,062.00	4,43,724.00
23.	Jiwaji	9,31,300.00	6,20,867.00	5,40,000.00
24.	Karnatak	6,31,337.00	4,08,771.00	4,09,104.00
25.	Kashmir	—	—	5,00,000.00
26.	Kerala	12,78,000.00	8,52,000.00	6,50,000.00
27.	Kurukshetra	9,00,000.00	6,00,000.00	5,90,000.00
28.	Lucknow	4,80,950.00	3,20,620.00	58,000.00
29.	Madras	8,60,450.00	5,73,634.00	6,20,000.00
30.	Madurai	—	—	1,50,000.00

Contd.

ANNEXURE 3.1 Contd.

1	2	3	4	5
31.	Magadh	8,00,000.00	5,33,000.00	2,00,000.00
32.	Marathwada	10,13,153.00	6,75,435.00	6,52,928.00
33.	Meerut	8,00,000.00	5,33,333.00	4,00,000.00
34.	Mysore	13,62,401.00	9,08,327.00	11,05,500.00
35.	Nagpur	9,51,000.00	4,75,550.00	4,90,550.00
36.	North Bengal	8,00,000.00	5,33,333.00	3,50,000.00
37.	Osmania	14,73,000.00	9,81,966.00	9,60,000.00
38.	Punjab	30,45,000.00	20,49,667.00	15,42,667.00
39.	Patna	13,59,474.00	9,06,317.00	8,75,000.00
40.	Poona	10,09,000.00	6,72,333.00	6,35,000.00
41.	Punjabi	11,80,000.00	7,86,666.00	6,65,000.00
42.	Rabindra Bharati	—	—	2,10,000.00
43.	Rajasthan	16,60,919.00	11,27,216.00	7,60,000.00
44.	Ranchi	10,50,500.00	7,00,000.00	—
45.	Ravishanker	7,65,000.00	5,10,000.00	5,35,000.00
46.	Roorkee	8,94,922.00	5,96,614.00	6,04,133.00
47.	Sardar Patel	10,41,187.00	6,94,125.00	6,62,000.00
48.	Saugar	8,43,554.00	5,53,569.00	5,27,290.66
49.	Saurashtra	—	—	3,45,000.00
50.	Shivaji	7,71,835.00	4,00,000.00	4,22,976.00
51.	SNDT	8,46,532.00	5,64,000.00	1,70,400.00
52.	South Gujarat	—	—	2,50,000.00
53.	Sri Venkateswara	14,65,000.00	7,76,666.00	7,50,667.00
54.	Utkal	8,94,630.00	5,94,420.00	5,85,220.00
55.	Varsaneya Sanskrit	8,01,462.00	5,33,333.00	6,10,000.00
56.	Vikram	10,09,785.00	5,32,942.00	5,09,000.00
57.	Visva Bharati	10,03,100.00	10,03,100.00	11,05,400.00
	Institutions deemed as University			
58.	Gujarat Vidyapeeth	5,00,000.00	3,33,333.00	2,65,000.00
59.	Gurukul Kangri	—	—	15,000.00
60.	IIS Bangalore	19,35,100.00	19,35,100.00	19,16,000.00
61.	Jamia Millia	5,70,450.00	3,33,334.00	3,70,000.00
62.	Kashi Vidyapeeth	5,00,000.00	3,33,333.00	3,75,000.00
63.	Tata Inst. of Social Sciences	30,000.00	30,000.00	25,000.00

ANNEXURE 3.2

Standards for Library Buildings and Design

Based on IS : 1553-1976–Indian Standard Recommendation relating to Primary Elements in the Design of Library Buildings. (First Revision)

1. Location
   The library should be centrally located with reference to buildings of faculties and departments, laboratories and hostels.

2. Rooms to be provided are as follows:

Sl.No.	Rooms Normally Separate	Academic library*	
		UCL*	UDL**
1	2	3	4
(i)	Stack Room	R	—
(ii)	Catalogue Room	R	—
(iii)	General Reading Room	R	R
(iv)	Periodical Reading Room	R	—
(v)	Special Reading Room	R	—
(vi)	Research Cubicles	R	—
(vii)	Group Study Room	R	—
(viii)	Seminar Room	R	—
(ix)	Conference Room	—	—
(x)	Exhibition Room	R	—
(xi)	Librarian's Room	R	—
(xii)	Deputy Librarian's Room	R	—
(xiii)	Technical Staff Room	R	—
(xiv)	Administrative Staff Room	R	—
(xv)	Committee Room	R	—
(xvi)	Display Room	R	—
(xvii)	Night Watchman's Room	R	—

Contd.

TABLE *Contd.*

1	2	3	4
(xviii)	Microfilm Reading Room	R	—
(xix)	Document Reproduction Room		
(xx)	Audio Visual Room	—	—
(xxi)	Store Room	R	R

* University Central Library.
** University/College Departmental Library.

3.0 Stack Room

3.1 Dimensions of Stack Room should be as follows:

(a) *Clear Length* in metres–1.80 n+3.10 where *n* is the number of rows of book racks*

(b) *Clear Width*

(1) 3 m (on the basis of one rack 2 m long plus one longitudinal gangway of 1 m) close to a longitudinal wall,
(2) 5 m (on the basis of 2 racks each 2 m long plus longitudinal gangway of 1 m) close to a longitudinal wall,
(3) 8 m (on the basis of 3 racks each 2 m long plus two longitudinal gangways of 1 m each) close to each of the longitudinal walls, and
(4) 10 m (on the basis of 4 racks each 2 m long plus two longitudinal gangways of 1 m each) close to each to the longitudinal walls.

* Each unit rack 2 m long may be assumed to house 700 to 750 volumes and I m^2 of stack room area may be assumed to house 150 volumes.

Note: 1 The centre to centre distance between consecutive racks is 1.80 m. (on the basis of 0.45 m of rack depth plus 1.35 m of cross gangway width).

Note: 2 The distance from an end wall of the stack room to the centre of the nearest row of rack is 1.55 m (on the basis of 1.325 m of the end cross gangway plus 0.225 m of half rack depth).

Note: Three metres and five metres widths are generally only in case of stack spaces, as the stack room and the reading room may be combined into a single room, in such cases.

(c) *Clear Height*–Floor to ceiling, 2.40 m.**

3.2 Stack room should be so oriented as to avoid direct sun.

4.0 **Windows**

4.1 Stack room-windows in the side walls of the stackroom should be opposite each cross gangway.

4.2 Each window should be provided with glass shutters and protected with wire fabric having its aperture sufficiently small to prevent squirrels, rats, etc., from getting in. In its fully open position the glass shutter should not project into the gangway.

4.3 Other Rooms–All windows and ventilators in the rooms accessible from outside should be provided with wire fabric to prevent books, pamphlets, etc. being passed out through them.

5.0 **Sizes of Rooms**

5.1 Reading Room–The average area per reader in the reading room should be 2.33 m^2, minimum.

Note–The size of the reading table as shown in this report is 2.4×0.6 m. the centre to centre distance between two consecutive rows of reading room tables is 1.8 m with seating arrangement on one side of the table only.

5.2 Sizes of other rooms shall normally be as follows:

	For use of	Area M^2
(a)	Librarian and deputy librarian	30
(b)	Classifier, Cataloguer, accession librarian and maintenance librarian	9 per person
(c)	Secretary to the librarian	19
(d)	Visitor's room	15
(e)	Administrative and professional staff not at service points and other than those mentioned in (b)	5 per person
(f)	Group discussion room	2 per person
(g)	Conference room	2 per person
(h)	Seminar room	2 per person
(i)	Committee room	2 per person
(j)	Cubicles	7 per person

** *Note*: 1. The height of the rack is ?.20 m and allovance for bay guide is 0.20 m.
Note: 2. The stack room should be combined with necessary devices for effective ventilation.

6.0 Libraries of all types are expanding at an enormous rate. Increase in demand for documents, official policy and increase in literacy make this process inevitable. Since the development of new libraries takes several years, the stock to be accommodated on the opening day, therefore, will be larger than was estimated when planning started. Therefore, it is absolutely essential to estimate the areas of the library at a given future date and relate the requirements to that date.

7.0 **Circulation**

7.1 Each floor of the library building shall be at one single level to facilitate the movement of book trolley from one part to another. Thresholds shall not be provided anywhere inside the building.

7.1.1. The movement of the book trolley from one tier to another, where there are three or more tiers in the stackroom, should be through electric lifts provided within the stackroom with landing at every tier of the stackroom and at other connected adjacent rooms. In large libraries where quick mechanical carriage of books and related materials are required, special arrangements, such as pneumatic tubes and belt conveyers, may become necessary. This may require to be considered at the initial stages of design of the library and its building.

7.1.2. The rooms shall be arranged in such a way that the staff other than those servicing the reading room shall not have to pass through the reading room disturbing the readers.

8.0 **Relative Position of Rooms**

8.1 The stack room should be so placed that it is easily accessible from and proximate to every part of the library.

8.2 The catalogue room should be like an ante-room to the stack room on the way from the general reading room to the stack room.

8.3 The general reading room should be close to the entrance.

8.4 Periodicals rooms may be further removed from the general reading room. But independent access to it shall be possible when the other rooms in the library are closed.

8.5 Special reading rooms may be still further removed from the general reading room.

8.6 The librarian or the deputy librarian should have his room in close proximity to the general reading room.

8.7 The rooms of the technical and administrative staff should be placed in close proximity to the rooms of the librarian and the deputy librarian.

8.8 The technical staff shall have independent access to the stack and catalogue areas.

8.9 The cubicles, the rooms for group study, the committee room, etc. may be in a separate wing or a separate floor.

8.10 The exhibition room may be combined with the entrance lobby or placed as close to it as possible.

9.0 The furniture and fittings for library shall be as per IS: 1829 (parts I and II) and IS: Library furniture and fittings: Part I Timber (First Revision) and Part II Steel and IS : 3663-1981 dimensions for rigid couplings. Tables and Chairs for general office purpose.

10.0 Requirement for fitment for drainage and sanitation for library building shall be as per the table enclosed.

Libraries-Based on IS : 1972-1983 Indian Standard Code of Basic Requirements for Water Supply, Drainage and Sanitation (Third Revision)

Art Galleries, Libraries & Museums

Sl. No.	Fitments	For male public	For female public	For male staff	For female staff
(1)	(2)	(3)	(4)	(5)	(6)
(i)	Water-closets	1 per 200 persons up to 400 persons; and for over 400 persons, add at the rate of 1 per 250 persons or part thereof	1 per 100 persons up to 200 persons and for over 200 persons, add at the rate of 1 per 150 persons or part thereof	1 for 1 to 15 persons 2 for 16 to 35 persons	1 for 1 to 12 persons 2 for 13 to 25 persons
(ii)	Ablution taps	1 in each water-closet	1 in each water-closet	1 in each water-closet	1 in each water-closet
			1 water tap with draining arrangements shall be provided for every 50 persons or part thereof in the vicinity of water-closets and urinals		

(*Contd.*)

TABLE (*Contd.*)

(1)	(2)	(3)	(4)	(5)	(6)
(iii)	Urinals	1 per 50 persons		Nil up to 6 persons 1 for 7 for 20 persons 2 for 21 to 45 persons	
(iv)	Wash Basins	1 for every 200 persons or part thereof; and for over 400 persons add at the rate of 1 per 250 person or part thereof	1 for every 200 persons or part thereof; and for every 200 persons add at the rate of 1 per 150 persons or part thereof	1 for 1 to 15 persons 2 for 15 to 35 persons	1 for 1 to 12 persons 2 for 13 to 25 persons
(v)	Cleaner's Sinks	———		1 per floor, Min ———	
(iv)	Drinking water + fountain	———		1 per 100 persons or part thereof	

ANNEXURE 4.1

Chief Recommendations of Ranganathan Committee (1965) on Book Selection and Book Purchase

Ranganathan Committee (1965) Chief Recommendations

2. The authority concerned may make the allocation of the amount for the purchase of reading materials as indicated in Sec. 23, items 4 and 8 of the report.

2.1 The proportion implied in the allocation should normally be continued for at least three years without undue disturbance unless there are unexpected special factors coming into play. The proportion may be reviewed and re-established periodically, say once in three years;

3. The authority concerned should provide a panel of experts in different subjects to help the librarian in making the final selection of reading and kindred materials;

4. It should be regarded as improper to call for tenders or competitive quotations for each order;

5. Standing vendors may be appointed with stipulated terms including discount and exchange rate for a year or a longer period with a clause in the agreement that if orders are not filled within a prescribed period the librarian will be free to place orders with others. In this, special weight should be given to advanced books and treatises;

6. Within the limits of the policy laid down, and in conformity to the advice of the experts concerned, and without exceeding the sanctioned budget and allocation, the librarian should be entrusted with the responsibility of book-selection and the acquisition of reading and kindred materials;

7. The authority concerned may exercise the power of review to satisfy itself that the acquisition of reading and kindred materials was being done without infringement of the policy and the limitations of the budget and the allocation, and for watching for factors needing amendment in the policy and in

the allocation of the fund;

32. To minimise the harmful effect of the practices in vogue in the choice of *ad hoc* or standing vendors for the supply of books, such as:
    1. Leading to failure of prompt supply of nascent books;
    2. By-passing of the supply of advanced books and treatises in limited demand, of difficult-to-get-at kinds and without an attractive trade discount; and
    3. Resulting in the ultimate lapse of budget allotment for books or for its diversion at the last minute to less important books because of their being available on the spot;

    It is necessary to rationalise the vendor-library relation as it is now only in a formative stage.
33. To facilitate this and reach an agreed standard, such as net-book agreement, which will not either stifle the development of a healthy book trade or vitiate the proper utilisation of the book-fund of the libraries, it would be desirable for the Commission to bring about a conference consisting of a few representatives of publishers, book-sellers, the library profession, the top-management of universities, and if feasible, representatives of Statutory Library Authorities in areas in which a Library Act is in force.
34. In view of the increasing cost of foreign books, it is desirable for the Commission to promote publication of cheap Indian editions of foreign books in wide demand in the universities and colleges or their import in sheets and being bound in India.
35. To minimise the effect of the:
    1. Present exchange difficulties;
    2. Import licence difficulties; and
    3. Frustrating delay caused by these two factors in the procurement of foreign reading materials,

    It is desirable for the Commission,

either

To arrange through a suitable agency for:

1. Poling together the orders of the different libraries for foreign reference books and advanced treatises of too limited a demand to warrant cheap Indian edition or Indian binding;

2. Their purchase in bulk; and
3. Their distribution to the libraries and debiting of their cost against the grant due to the respective libraries.

or

To give part of the grant in the form of foreign exchange licence or coupons.

35. If the first alternative is followed, to minimise the danger of cooperative or centralised purchases resulting in the curtailment of the freedom of libraries in book-selection, the Commission may adopt special methods such as the following:
    1. Appoint an Expert Committee for each subject to make a book selection list of reference books and advanced treatises, likely to be needed by many universities and colleges;
    2. Circulate these lists to the libraries of the universities and bigger colleges for their respective selection;
    3. Consolidate the returns on these lists for bulk purchase;

Such lists in the different subjects may go out at different times. They may also be promoted by the libraries corresponding among themselves. This device may be given up as soon as the current difficult situation in respect of foreign exchange and import licence disappears.

ANNEXURE 4.2

Use of Library Books by Teachers and Students as appeared in Standards of University Education — UGC Report, 1965

Name of the university	Number of books issued to students	Number of students (1962-63)	Number of books issued to every 10 students	Number of books issued to teachers	Number of teachers in the university teaching departments/ university colleges (1962-63)	Total number of books issued in the university library (2)+(5)	Total number of borrowers (3)+(6)
1	2	3	4	5	6	7	8
1. Agra University (Central Library)	320	554	6	289	32	609	586
2. Allahabad University	1781	8462	2	179	278	1960	8740
3. Annamalai University	1245	3182	4	801	265	2046	3447
4. Bihar University	—	6094	—	—	257	232	6351
5. Calcutta University	4285	9132	5	431	628	4716	9760
6. Delhi University	—	5518	—	—	344	6294	5862
7. Gauhati University	700	1999	4	140	112	840	2111
8. Gorakhpur University	640	3586	2	60	194	700	3780
9. Gurukul Kangri Vishvavidyalaya	340	—	—	149	—	489	—
10. Jabalpur University	222	464	5	96	22	318	486
11. Jadavpur University	480	3621	1	360	299	840	3920
12. Jammu & Kashmir University	800	355	23	200	42	1000	397
13. Kalyani University	155	470	3	57	48	212	518
14. Karnatak University	206	2501	1	206	193	412	2694

(Contd.)

1	2	3	4	5	6	7	8
15. Kerala University	—	189	—	—	44	495	233
16. Kurukshetra University	319	758	4	64	52	383	810
17. Madras University	—	988	—	—	146	1954	1134
18. Marathwada University	210	420	5	73	12	283	432
19. M.S. University of Baroda	—	10106	—	—	432	7335	10538
20. Mysore University	1089	3898	3	195 **	283	1284	4181
21. Nagpur University	1017	1545	7	200	98	1217	1643
22. North Bengal University	—	—	—	—	—	200	—
23. Osmania University	1571	12660	1	170	753	1741	13413
24. Panjab University	2104	3573	6	525	217	2629	3790
25. Patna University	2958	10815	3	158	590	3116	11405
26. Poona University	5000	888	56	688	63	5688	951
27. Rabindra Bharati	200	131	15	50	31	250	162
28. Rajasthan University	—	6905	—	—	311	1980	7216
29. S.V. Vidyapeeth	—	588	—	—	51	370	639
30. Saugar University	730	2449	3	107	150	837	2599
31. S.N.D.T. Women's University	349	2467	1	111	136	460	2603
32. Sri Venkateswara University	652	1135	6	221	142	873	1277
33. Varsaneya Sanskrit Vishvavidyalaya	235	—	—	79	—	314	—
34. Vikram University	889	2384	4	75	106	964	2490
35. Viswa Bharati*	620	490	13	350	115	970	605

* Books issued for reference in the library are not included.

** Including registered graduates.

ANNEXURE 4.3

UGC Grants to the Universities for the Purchase of Library Books and Periodicals till 31st March, 1973

Sl. No.	University	First Plan	Second Plan	Third Plan	Fourth Plan
1	2	3	4	5	6
1.	Agra	60,000	2,95,000	2,08,000	5,15,378
2.	Aligarh	1,50,000	4,98,000	6,05,000	16,70,396
3.	Allahabad	1,80,000	4,27,600	6,32,000	9,84,628
4.	Andhra	1,55,000	3,72,000	1,90,000	13,41,131
5.	Annamalai	95,000	3,13,334	3,05,000	11,24,388
6.	BHU	1,25,000	2,96,000	3,10,556	24,18,882
7.	Bangalore	—	—	50,000	10,17,791
8.	Baroda	1,00,000	5,23,6000	3,65,886	15,58,107
9.	Berhampur	—	—	—	3,95,878
10.	Bhagalpur	—	5,000	2,55,000	7,84,789
11.	Bhopal	—	—	—	40,000
12.	Bihar	1,20,000	3,83,300	3,85,000	8,86,065
13.	Bombay	90,000	3,27,500	2,83,082	17,41,723
14.	Burdwan	—	—	2,45,000	13,07,378
15.	Calcutta	1,30,000	4,25,000	2,19,000	16,86,462
16.	Calicut	—	—	—	10,39,351
17.	Cochin	—	—	—	40,000
18.	Delhi	1,80,000	6,04,500	4,27,400	7,81,128
19.	Dibrugarh	—	—	—	4,80,378
20.	Gauhati	90,000	4,65,000	3,45,000	12,55,383
21.	Gorakhpur	—	3,50,000	1,71,000	7,32,499
22.	Gujarat	1,10,000	4,70,000	4,27,000	8,76,149
23.	Guru Nanak Dev	—	—	—	3,40,000
24.	Himachal	—	—	—	2,70,000
25.	Indrakala	—	—	—	10,000
26.	Indore	—	—	35,000	8,30,681
27.	Jabalpur	—	1,00,000	6,59,000	4,39,378
28.	Jadavpur	—	3,41,000	3,67,903	11,24,062
29.	Jammu	92,000	1,68,000	4,62,000	3,99,973
30.	JNU (Delhi)	—	—	—	5,40,000
31.	Jiwaji	—	—	75,000	6,46,256
32.	Jodhpur	—	—	3,20,880	9,77,375
33.	Kalyani	—	—	2,40,000	7,60,378
34.	Kanpur	—	—	—	1,80,378
35.	Karnatak	1,40,000	95,000	4,80,000	8,45,382
36.	Kashmir	—	—	—	6,61,237
37.	Kerala	1,10,000	2,51,000	6,14,097	15,12,378

Contd.

ANNEXURE 4.3 — Contd.

1 2	3	4	5	6
38. Kurukshetra	—	—	4,00,000	5,96,378
39. Lucknow	95,000	4,86,000	4,10,000	7,45,693
40. Madras	1,00,000	3,80,000	3,32,667	15,70,340
41. Madurai	—	—	—	4,61,578
42. Magadh	—	—	1,10,000	4,36,204
43. Marathwada	—	1,80,000	2,75,000	7,72,378
44. Meerut	—	—	—	6,65,378
45. Mysore	95,000	2,20,000	5,29,500	11,25,311
46. Nagpur	66,500	1,30,000	5,85,312	10,68,322
47. North Bengal	—	—	2,70,000	2,65,378
48. Osmania	1,85,000	3,40,000	4,20,333	14,44,082
49. Patna	70,000	1,60,000	3,95,400	16,34,820
50. Poona	90,000	2,98,300	3,06,400	11,18,600
51. Punjab	50,000	4,40,000	10,29,010	18,64,617
52. Punjabi	—	—	2,50,000	5,10,378
53. Rabindra Bharti	—	—	11,000	2,70,000
54. Rajasthan	65,000	4,89,000	6,57,100	12,63,124
55. Ranchi	—	—	3,37,000	5,84,536
56. Ravishanker	—	—	40,000	5,78,952
57. Roorkee	40,000	73,750	2,71,250	16,66,382
58. Sambalpur	—	—	—	7,12,878
59. Sardar Patel	—	3,10,000	3,50,000	8,65,378
60. Saugar	1,30,000	4,12,100	3,81,753	12,46,130
61. Saurashtra	—	—	—	6,31,878
62. Shivaji	—	—	1,00,000	8,34,878
63. SNDT	30,000	70,000	2,45,000	6,05,876
64. South Gujarat	—	—	—	8,28,094
65. Sri Venkateswara	75,000	2,81,000	2,30,000	5,64,196
66. Udaipur	—	—	40,000	9,35,432
67. Utkal	85,000	2,85,000	2,15,000	11,19,828
68. Varasaneya Sanskrit	—	50,000	1,95,000	35,000
69. Vikram	—	1,20,000	4,45,500	6,76,806
70. Visva Bharti	10,000	1,50,000	2,70,000	7,65,378
Institutions Deemed as University				
71. BITS	—	—	—	6,14,727
72. Gujarat Vidyapeeth	—	—	60,000	2,85,000
73. Gurukul Kangri	—	—	2,12,000	2,08,000
74. Indian Inst. of Science	—	—	1,84,000	11,74,334
75. Indian School of Mines	—	—	—	1,33,583
76. Jamia Millia	—	—	71,500	3,99,859
77. Kashi Vidyapeeth	—	—	60,000	3,45,000
78. Tata Inst. of Social Sciences	—	—	15,000	1,80,000

ANNEXURE 5.1

UGC Expert Committee – Report on the Minimum Qualifications on Workload etc. for Librarians (1967)

1. Background

The University Grants Commission appointed a Committee on December 24, 1983 under the chairmanship of Professor R.C. Mehrotra, Emeritus Professor, Rajasthan University, Jaipur to consider the revision of pay scales, career/professional development and service conditions of teachers in the universities and colleges.

In October, 1985 the Commission in consultation with the Government of India, requested the Committee to consider the revision of pay scales of Librarians and Directors of Physical Education, in addition to the pay scales of university and college teachers.

The report of the Committee on revision of pay scales of Librarians and Directors of Physical Education in universities and colleges has been submitted to the Commission on 3rd September, 1986.

The main recommendations/observations of the Committee are as follows:

> "The Committee noted that the principle of parity has been established in the matter of scales of pay between university and college teachers and Librarians and Directors/Instructors of Physical Education in the universities and colleges. In the case of teachers, the Committee has recommended pay scales in the existing framework; the same may be applied to pay scales of these categories. These pay scales may, therefore, be treated as notional and would have to be converted in the light of the recommendations of the Fourth Pay Commission. The Committee recommends that while converting these scales, it should be ensured that the Librarians and Directors/Instructors of Physical Education in universities and colleges are not put to any financial disadvantage and envisaged parity is maintained."

Recommendations for Librarians' Pay scales

The pay scales recommended for the various categories of Librarians in universities and colleges are as follows:

Universities	*Pay scale in the existing framework Rs.*
(i) Asstt. University Librarian/ Documentation Officer	700-40-1100-50-1600
(ii) Asstt. University Librarian (Senior scale)/Documentation Officer (Senior scale)	1200-50-1300-60-1900
(iii) Asstt. University Librarian (Selection grade)/Documentation Officer (Selection grade)	2000-125/2-2250
(iv) Deputy University Librarian	1500-60-1800-100-2000-125/2-2250
(v) University Librarian	1800-100-2000-125/2 2750-125-3000

Colleges

(i) College Librarian	700-40-1100-50-1600
(ii) College Librarian (Senior scale)	1200-50-1300-60-1900
(iii) College Librarian (Selection grade)	2000-125/2-2250

Selection procedure

Selection for the post of University Librarian, Deputy University Librarian, Assistant University Librarian/College Librarian/-Documentation Officer should be made strictly on merit on an All India basis. The Selection Committee should include atleast two experts not connected with the university. Promotion of candidates to the senior scale and selection grade should also be done on the recommendations of a Selection Committee having atleast one expert not connected with the university.

Probation

An Assistant University Librarian, Dy. University Librarian, University Librarian, College Librarian and Director of Physical Instructions and Sports may normally be put on probation for a period of two years.

The Librarians should be treated as non-vacation staff and entitled to the leave admissible to other non-vacation staff in universities. The working hours of Librarians will conform to the library timings. During the vacations, the Librarians should participate in programmes for their professional development.

Age of Superannuation

The Committee recommends that the age of superannuation of the Librarians may continue to be 60 years. No extension or re-employment be given.

Code of Conduct

The Committee had recommended a Code of Ethics for the teachers in Part 'A' of the report. The recommendations regarding this may be suitably modified in the case of Librarians keeping in view the duties to be assigned to them.

The basic recommendations of the Committee relate to : (a) scales of pay, (b) avenues of promotion, and (c) conditions of service. The Committee suggested the constitution of two Expert Committees. The Expert Committees may be requested to pay special attention to the following:

(i) *Minimum qualifications*
  (a) for open All India recruitment at different levels;
  (b) for promotion to higher grades within the same cadre; and
  (c) for completion of satisfactory period of probation.

(ii) Specific items to be included in the self-appraisal and evaluation forms;

(iii) Facilities for professional training and development, taking into account the expansion of activities and augmentation of refresher courses and tests,

(iv) Workload to be defined, specifically to meet the special nature of their duties and functions (i.e. staggering of hours etc.).

The Commission at its meeting held on 27th October, 1986 considered the report and generally agreed with the recommendations of the Committee relating to : (a) scales of pay, (b) avenues of promotion, and (c) conditions of service. The Commission desired that an Expert Committee may be appointed to consider the minimum qualifications and workload etc., as envisaged in para 1.5.

Composition

In view of the above decision of the Commission, an Expert Committee was constituted consisting of ten members under the Chairmanship of Prof. G. Padmanabhan with the following terms of reference.

Terms of Reference

The terms of reference of the Committee is to consider further the recommendations of the Committee on revision of pay scales of Librarians in universities and colleges (Mehrotra Committee Report Part 'B') on the following matters:

(i) *Minimum qualifications*

  (a) for open All India recruitment at different levels;
  (b) for promotion to higher grades within the same cadre; and
  (c) for completion of satisfactory period of probation;

(ii) Specific items to be included in the self-appraisal and evaluation forms;

(iii) Facilities for professional training and development, taking into account the expansion of activities and augmentation of refresher courses and tests;

(iv) Workload to be defined, specifically to meet the special nature of their duties and functions (i.e. staggering of hours etc.).

Librarians

The Committee made following recommendations for various categories of librarian's qualification.

Assistant University Librarian/College Librarian/ Documentation Officer

The minimum qualifications recommended for the post of Assistant University Librarian/College Librarian/Documentation Officer are as follows:

(i) Qualifying at the national test conducted for the purpose by the UGC or any other agency approved the by the UGC.
(ii) Master's degree in Library Science/Information Science/ Documentation or an equivalent professional degree with atleast fifty-five per cent marks or its equivalent grade plus a consistently good academic record.

OR

Master's degree in the Arts/Science/Commerce or equivalent degree with atleast fifty-five per cent marks or its equivalent grade and a Bachelor's degree in Library Science/Information Science/Documentation or an equivalent professional degree with atleast fifty-five per cent marks or its equivalent grade plus a consistently good academic record.

Assistant University Librarian (senior scale)/College Librarian (senior scale)/Documentation Officer (senior scale)

An Assistant University Librarian/College Librarian/Documentation Officer may be considered for promotion to Assistant University Librarian/College Librarian/Documentation Officer (senior scale) Rs. 1200-1900 after completing eight years of service as an Assistant University Librarian/College Librarian/Documentation Officer or on reaching a basic pay of Rs. 1020 and having the following minimum qualifications:

(i) Master's degree in Library Science/Information Science/ Documentation or one year course of specialisation in an area of information technology/Archive and manuscript keeping or Master's degree in an area of thrust in the institution;
(ii) Should have attended atleast two summer institutes or refresher courses or orientation course of about five weeks' duration each with proper and well-defined evaluation procedure; and
(iii) Consistently good appraisal reports.

An Assistant University Librarian/College Librarian/Documentation Officer would cease to earn his annual increments beyond Rs. 1300 in case he does not acquire the following minimum qualifications:

(i) Master's degree in Library Science/Information Science/

Documentation *or* One year course of specialisation in an area of information technology/Archive and manuscript keeping *or* Master's degree in an area of thrust in the institution.

Assistant University Librarian/College Librarian/ Documentation Officer (Selection Grade)

An Assistant University Librarian/College Librarian/Documentation Officer (senior scale) could be promoted to Assistant University Librarian/College Librarian/Documentation Officer (selection grade) provided:

(i) he has reached the basic pay of Rs. 1900 in the scale of Rs. 1200-1900;
(ii) he has attended atleast two refresher courses or summer institutes or about five weeks' duration with proper and well defined evaluation procedure after his placement in the scale of Rs. 1200-1900; and
(iii) his performance appraisal reports are found satisfactory by the Selection Committee including atleast one outside expert.

Deputy University Librarian

(i) Master's Degree in Library Science/Information Science/ Documentation with atleast fifty-five per cent marks or its equivalent grade and a consistently good academic record;
(ii) One year specialisation in an area of information technology/ Archives and manuscript keeping or Master's degree in an area of thrust in the institution;
(iii) Seven years' experience as an Assistant University Librarian/ College Librarian, and
(iv) Evidence of innovative library services, published work and professional commitment.

Desirable

M.Phil./Ph.D. degree in Library Science/Information Science/ Documentation/Archives and manuscript keeping.

University Librarian

(i) Master's Degree in Library Science/Information Science/

Documentation with at least fifty-five per cent marks or its equivalent grade and a consistently good academic record;

(ii) One year specialisation in an area of information technology/ Archives and manuscript keeping or Master's Degree in an area of thrust in the institution;

(iii) Atleast eight years' service as a Deputy Librarian in a University Library or fifteen years experience as a College Librarian; and

(iv) Evidence of innovative library service and organisation of published work.

Desirable

M.Phil./Ph.D. degree in Library Science/Information Science/ Documentation/Archives and manuscript keeping.

Selection

The Committee recommended that the selection of Assistant University Librarian/College Librarian/Documentation Officer, Deputy University Librarian and University Librarian must be made on All India basis with the help of Selection Committee. The Selection Committee includes atleast two outside experts not connected with the university and one of them should be practicing Librarian.

Career Development of Existing Librarians

This Committee received many representations regarding pay revision given to Librarians with effect from 1st April, 1980. One of the qualifications proposed for the new scale of Rs. 700-1600 was first or second class B.A./B.Sc./B.Com. degree plus a first or second class M.Lib.Sc. degree or first or second class M.A./M.Sc./M.Com. degree and a first or second class B. Lib. Science or a diploma in Library Science. Those who were appointed before 1-1-1973 were given exception in respect of acquiring the new qualifications.

In the 1st January, 1973 revision while the scales of Rs. 400-500 and Rs. 400-800 were upgraded to Rs. 700-1300 and Rs. 700-1100 respectively, the scale of Rs. 300-600 was upgraded to Rs. 550-900. It appears that there are a small number of incumbents who have not got the Rs. 700-1600 grade in 1980 (especially the ones in Rs. 550-900), since they possess a Master's degree with a third class. These incumbents had no opportunity or facilities to improve their qualifications, it is claimed that they have large years of experience and some are on the verge of retirement. Therefore, it has been represented that relaxation in qualification should also be given to those appointed before 1st April, 1980 sine all the scales were merged into Rs. 700-1600 at this point of time.

The Committee recommends those who were appointed before 1st April, 1980 but having a qualification of Master's degree (III class) and Bachelor's degree/Diploma in Library Science, should also be given the grade of Rs. 700-1600, if they had put in atleast ten years of experience as Assistant Librarian/College Librarian/Documentation Officer by 1-4-80. However, these persons should obtain the prescribed additional professional qualifications in case they would like to be considered for higher posts.

The Committee felt that the posts of Deputy Librarian and Librarians may also be created in the selected colleges. The UGC evolve suitable criteria for selection of such colleges.

A provision should be made to award positions of Librarians of Eminence on the lines of Professors of Eminence for outstanding Librarians.

Probation

The Committee recommends that an Assistant University Librarian/ College Librarian/Documentation Officer, Deputy University Librarian and University Librarian may normally be put on probation for a period of two years.

An Assistant University Librarian/College Librarian/Documentation Officer may be confirmed only when he has actually completed a short term course of three-four weeks' duration in a relevant field and his performance appraisal reports are found satisfactory.

Recommendations Regarding Evaluation, Workload, Code of Conduct, Professional Training etc. for Librarians

Evaluation of Librarians

The importance of evaluation has been explained in the Mehrotra Committee report. The National Policy on Education and its Programme of Action has emphasised evaluation of teachers in the universities and colleges. The Committee is of the opinion that evaluation of Librarians in the universities and colleges is equally important. The Committee had appointed the Sub-Committees to suggest format for evaluation of Librarians. The format suggested is at Appendix III for Librarians.

Workload for Librarians

The Committee endorsed the recommendations of Mehrotra Committee report, para 'B' regarding workload for Librarians that:

> "The Librarians should be treated as non-vacation staff and entitled to the leave admissible to other non-vacation staff in universities. The working hours of Librarians will similarly conform to the library timings. During the vacations, the Librarians should participate in programmes for their professional development."

The Committee recommends that since the promotion of the Librarians is linked to acquisition of additional qualifications, they should be given the necessary facilities and every kind of leave (such as duty/sabbatical/study) admissible to teachers for career development and improvement of qualifications. It will help them in giving better services.

Code of Ethics

The Committee is of the view that code of ethics for Librarians formulated with the help of their National Level Organisation as suggested for teachers in Programme of Action of National Policy on Education, 1986.

Professional training for Librarians

Considering the rapid expansion in the information system and development of modern management techniques for running libraries, continuous professional training of Librarians has become essential. The Committee had appointed a sub-committee to identify the courses for continuous professional training of Librarians and the places where such courses could be conducted, as given in Appendix V of the report.

Self Assessment for College/University Directors of Physical Education, Sports and Librarians

1. (a) Name (in full block letters) ....
   (b) Age (Date of birth) ....
   (c) Designation ....
   (d) Department ....
   (e) Date of joining the present post ....
   (mention institution, if more than one) ....
   (f) Present post held and since when ....
   (g) Scale of pay and basic pay ....
   (h) Whether permanent/on probation ....
   (i) Leave taken during the year ....
   (mention type of leave and total no. of days) ....
2. Qualifications

	Year	*University/Institution*
(a) General		
(i)		
(ii)		
(iii)		
(iv)		
(b) Professional		
(i)		
(ii)		
(iii)		
(iv)		
(v)		
(vi)		

Format for Evaluation by Self, Peer and Reviewing Officer

Year ....

1. (a) Name (in full BLOCK LETTERS) ....
   (b) Designation ....
   (c) Date of birth ....
   (d) Department/Branch/Section ....
   (e) Date of joining this Institution's service ....
   (f) Present post held since ....
   (g) Scale of pay & basic pay ....

(h) Whether permanent/temporary/ad-hoc ....

(i) Leave enjoyed during the year (total) ....

2. Qualifications

(a) Academic

	Year	*University/Institution*
(i)		
(ii)		
(iii)		
(iv)		

Mention any special feature/award/credit etc.

(b) Professional qualifications

	Year	*University/Instution*
(i) Certificate		
(ii) Diploma		
(iii) B. Lib. Sc.		
(iv) M. Lib. Sc./MLISC		
(v) M. Phil/Ph.D.		

(any special feature/award/credit etc.)

(c) Improvement of qualification during the preceding one year (degree/diploma, short-term training/orientation course, etc.) academic/professional:

....

....

....

(d) Research work: any kind of Library survey, evaluation, analysis that has been formally submitted/during the period

....

....

....

(e) Research papers/monographs/books published during last year (Title published/Journal)

....

....

....

(f) Research in progress: (any research project undertaken/assigned connected with the library or otherwise. Please give the title of the project and time limit etc.)

....

....

(g) Seminar, conference, symposium, etc. attended (including paper contributed, capacity in which participated, e.g. resource person, Rapporteurs, presented paper etc.: with details)

....

....

(h) Membership of professional bodies with details

....

....

....

3. Duties and job specifications

(a) Total weekly working hours ....
(b) Work in shifts/daily working schedule ....
(c) No. of staff members you supervise ....
(d) Kinds of job you have performed during the last year indicating the rank order
    (a) Supervisory ....
    (b) Policy and Planning ....
    (c) administration ....
    (d) books, periodical section, etc. ....
    (e) documentation ....
    (f) cataloguing and classification filing of cards ....
    (g) acquisition ....
    (h) periodicals ....
    (i) reference & bibliographical activities ....

(j) circulation ....
(k) stock-maintenance (including funding) ....
(l) display, promotional work ....
(m) editing & publishing ....
(n) computer section ....
(o) reprographic work ....
(p) staff training ....
(q) attending the library users personally ....
(r) meeting conference ....
(s) Social and extension activities ....
(t) gift and exchange ....
(u) inter-library loan ....
(v) teaching/academic ....

Give some details, where possible

4. (a) Languages known,
   (b) Mention any significant contribution you have made to improve the: (a) Library services of your Institution, and (b) Development of Library Profession.

Signature Librarian

Date: ....

To be completed by peers

Indicate overall assessment of the work of the individual.

Signature.............

Date: Designation.........

To be completed by Reviewing Officer

1. Do you agree with the information given?
2. If not give justificatioin
3. Overall assessment of work

Orientation Programmes that may be run for College Librarians/Assistant Librarians/Deputy Librarians/Librarians in University Libraries

Level I Courses

Target Group: College Librarians/Assistant Librarians in universities – Duration 100 hours.

Course 1 (LI–1)

1. Library management:
   Personnel, fiscal, library material, building, furniture equipment. Operational functions: (a) job analysis, (b) work-flow, (c) workload, (d) Evaluation of work, (e) Time scheme, and (f) Records and Statistics.

Course 2 (LA–2)

Resource Development and Management:

(a) Collection Development
(b) Resource sharing
(c) Net-working
(d) Information processing and Organisation
(e) Non-book materials.

Course 3 (LA–3)

User studies:

(a) User survey
(b) Information gathering habits
(c) User Education and Training
(d) Assessment of information needs of users
(e) Information use promotion.

Course 4 (LI–4)

Computer Application:

1. System Analysis for computerization
2. Hardware selection
3. Library application Software
4. Automation for Library jobs:

   (a) Acquisition
   (b) Serial Control
   (c) Cataloguing
   (d) Office Management
   (e) Circulation
   (f) Bibliographical Information handling
   (g) Database creation.

Course 5 (LI–5)

Information Services and Products:

1. Reference Service
2. CAS
3. SDI
4. Information Systems
5. Reprographic Services

Level II (L II) Courses

Target Group : Deputy Librarians/Librarians–
Duration : 100 hours

Course 1 (L II-1) Information Technology (Advance Course)

(i) Computer applications–An introduction to computers. Computer organisation and architecture:

(a) Application of computers to Library and Information work, Global and national scenes. Software and hardware concepts, Operating systems, Large, mini, micro and personal computers, word processors. Different types of computer equipment useful in implementing data information systems, input-output devices, storage devices, etc.

(b) Bibliography and information handling

(c) Office management

(ii) Reprographic Services

(iii) Elements of Telecommunication.

Course 2 (L II-2) Advance Course in Library Management

(a) Policy formulation
(b) Planning–Physical and functional
(c) Scheduling and monitoring
(d) Control
(e) Modelling
(f) Project Proposal and Implementation
(g) Evaluation

Course 3 (L II-3) Communication

I. Written communication:

(a) Technical Report Writing
(b) Feasibility Studies
(c) Project Report

II. Public Relations:

(a) Rapport with the Academic Community
(b) Rapport with administration
(c) Rapport with professional, academic bodies, learned Societies and funding agencies

III. Audio Visual communication–use of educational technology aids

Course 4 (L II-4) Conservation and Preservation

(a) Library materials
(b) Archival Cells

Institutions identified to run the Orientation Courses (Levels I&II)

University Librarians and/or Departments of Library and Information Sciences

1. Jadavpur University, Calcutta
2. Bhagalpur University, Bhagalpur
3. Banaras Hindu University, Varanasi
4. University of Delhi, Delhi
5. Aligarh Muslim University, Aligarh
6. Punjab University, Chandigarh
7. University of Nagpur, Nagpur
8. S.N.D.T., Bombay
9. University of Poona, Poona
10. University of Bombay, Bombay
11. University of Hyderabad, Hyderabad
12. Utkal University, Bhubaneswar
13. University of Sagar, Sagar
14. University of Kerala, Trivandrum
15. University of Mysore, Mysore
16. University of Rajasthan, Jaipur
17. Gauhati University, Gauhati

Institutions

1. D.R.T.C. Bangalore
2. National Library, Calcutta
3. Central Secretariat, New Delhi
4. Physical Research Library, Ahmedabad
5. Indian Instt. of Science, Bangalore
6. N.A.S.S.D.O.C., New Delhi
7. I.I.T., Bombay
8. I.I.T., Baroda
9. BARC, Bombay
10. M.S. University of Baroda, Baroda
11. DESIDOC, New Delhi
12. Nehru Museum & Library, New Delhi
13. National Aeronautical Library, Bangalore
14. CFTRI, Mysore
15. NICDAD, Lucknow

ANNEXURE 5.2

List of Academic Staff Colleges

State	*University*
Andhra Pradesh	1. Andhra University, Waltair.
	2. Hyderabad University.
	3. Osmania University, Hyderabad.
	4. Sri Venkateswara University, Tirupati.
Assam	5. Gauhati University.
Bihar	6. Patna University.
	7. Ranchi University.
	8. Bihar University, Muzaffarpur.
Gujarat	9. Gujarat University, Ahmedabad.
	10. Saurashtra University, Rajkot.
Haryana	11. Kurukshetra University.
Karnataka	12. Mysore University.
	13. Karnataka University, Dharwar.
Kerala	14. Calicut University.
	15. Kerala University, Trivandrum.
M.P.	16. Devi Ahilya University, Indore.
	17. Dr. H.S. Gaur University, Sagar
	18. Rani Durgawati Vishawavidyalaya, Jabalpur.
Maharashtra	19. Bombay University.
	20. Marathwada University, Aurangabad.
	21. Nagpur University.
	22. Poona University, Puna.
Meghalaya	23. NEHU, Shillong.
Orissa	24. Utkal University, Bhubaneswar.
Punjab	25. Punjab University, Chandigarh.
	26. Guru Nanak Dev University, Amritsar.
Pondicherry	27. Pondicherry University.
Rajasthan	28. Jodhpur University.
	29. Rajasthan University, Jaipur.

Tamil Nadu	30. Bharatidasan University, Tiruchirapalli.
	31. Madras University.
	32. Madurai Kamraj University.
	33. Bharthiar University, Coimbatore.
Uttar Pradesh	34. Aligarh Muslim University.
	35. Banaras Hindu University.
	36. Allahabad University.
	37. Lucknow University.
	38. Gorakhpur University.
West Bengal	39. Calcutta University.
	40. Visva Bharati, Santiniketan.
	41. Burdwan University.
	42. Jadavpur University, Calcutta.
Union Territory of Delhi	43. Delhi University.
	44. Jawaharlal Nehru University, New Delhi.
	45. Jamia Millia Islamia, New Delhi.
Goa	46. Goa University.
Himachal Pradesh	47. Himachal Pradesh University, Shimla.
Jammu & Kashmir	48. Kashmir University, Srinagar.

ANNEXURE 5.3

Syllabus and Sample Questions on Library & Information Science – Net Programme, UGC 1989

LIBRARY & INFORMATION SCIENCE

There are two papers, namely Paper - II and Paper - III. Syllabus for these two papers has been designed. Paper-II carries 100 marks, It consists of 50 multiple choice type questions, each carrying 2 marks.

Paper - III carries 200 marks and consists of short essay type questions. Duration of Paper - II generally be of $1^1/_2$ hours. Paper - III of 2 hours duration.

SYLLABUS
PAPER - II

Information, Communication, Library and Society

1. Information and Information Science.
2. Communication-Barriers, Models, Library/Information Centres as communication agencies.
3. Laws of Library Science.
4. Resource Sharing and Networking.
5. Library Movement and Legislation.
6. Types of libraries and their organisation.
7. Extension Services and Publicity.
8. Library and Information Profession and Associations.

Information Sources and Services

9. Primary, Secondary and Tertiary Sources.
10. Users Studies.
11. Users Education.
12. Library and Information Services – Reference Service, Current Awareness Service, Selective Dissemination of Information, Indexing and Abstracting Services, Digest Service, Data Service, Trend Report, Data Bases and Data Bank, Referral

Service and Search Strategies.
13. Translation Services – Tools and Pools.
14. Reprographic Services and Techniques.

Library Information Processing and Retrieval Techniques

15. Organisation of Knowledge/Information.
16. Classification – Modes of formation of subjects; Modes of thinking; Mapping of Universe of subjects of different schemes of classification – DC, UDC and CC: Canons and Principles.
17. Cataloguing: Normative Principles – Laws and canons: Cataloguing codes: Design and development – CCC and AACR I and II.
18. Indexing – Techniques, Subject indexing systems and procedures – Pre-coordinate and Post-coordinate Indexing, Chain indexing, KWIC, POPSI and PRECIS, Citation Indexing, Subject Heading List and Thesaurus.

Library and Information Management

19. Principles, practices and techniques of Scientific Management.
20. Schools of Thought.
21. Governance of Library and Information Centres.
22. Systems approach and analysis.
23. Planning, organisational structure.
24. Personnel management.
25. Financial management.
26. Performance measurement.
27. Physical environment – Building and equipment.

Information Technology, Information Systems and Programmes

28. Basics of computers – Hardware, Software, Humanware : Housekeeping operations and other services in libraries.
29. National and International Information Systems, Programmes and Agencies – INSDOC, NASSDOC, DESIDOC, SENDOC, UNESCO, IFLA, FID, UNISIST.
30. National and International Information Networks – Planning, Designing and Evaluation – NICNET, INDONET, INFLIBNET, CALIBNET, EURONET, BLAISE, OCLC, RLIN, MEDLARS, INIS, AGRIS.

Research and Statistical Methods

31. Research – Types of Research/Levels of research.
32. Scientific Method.
33. Research Design.
34. Research Methods: Historical Case Study, Descriptive, Comparative Statistical.
35. Research tools, techniques and operations.
36. Data analysis, consolidation and reporting.

PAPER - III

Information, Communication, Library and Society

	Topic	*Annotation*
1.	Information, Communication, social, Information Science and Library	Concept, need and purpose, Barriers cultural, educational and economic role of libraries
2.	Library Profession and Association	India, U.K., U.S.A. and International
3.	Library Movement and Legislation	India
4.	Library and Information Systems	National, Public, Academic and Special Libraries
5.	Library Extension Service and Publicity	Concept, need and purpose, planning programmes for promoting library use
5(a)	Resource Sharing & Networking	Concept, need, purpose, programmes problems UBC, UAP

Information and Reference Service

6.	Information and Reference Service	Concept, need and purpose
7.	Types of Information Services	Reference service, Current Awareness Service, Selective Dissemination of Information, Abstracting Service, Indexing Service, Digest Service, State of Art, Trend Report, Referral Service
8.	Search Strategies	Need and purpose
9.	Translation Service	Tools and Pools
10.	Reprographic Services	Concept, Methods and Techniques
11.	Automated Information Sources and services	Data Banks and Data Bases
12.	Users Study	Concept, need, purpose, techniques and methods
13.	Users Education	Concept, need, purpose, techniques and methods.

Library Information Processing and Retrieval Techniques

14. Classification	Current development, Trends and Research, Automation Schemes
15. Cataloguing	Current Developments, Trends and Research, Automation Standardisation Codes.
16. Indexing	Current Developments, Trends and Research, Automation, Standardisation, Evaluation Techniques.
17. Thesaurus	Concept, Construction, Thesaurofacet, Current developments, Trends and Research, Automation

Library and Information Management

18. Scientific Management	Concept, Application in Library and Information Management
19. Schools of Thought	Classical, Human Behaviour, Social System, Decision-Making
20. Systems Concept	Concept and components, Systems analysis, design, evaluation and implementation.
21. Planning and Decision-Making	Concept, Factors, Methodology steps. Management by objectives, Decision-making; nature, steps, process, problems and analysis.
22. Organisation	Structure and types
23. Personnel Management	Human relations, staffing, selection, quantification, development, motivation, job satisfaction and evaluation.
24. Financial Management	Library finance and budgeting its techniques.
25. Evaluation	Standards, Time and Motion Study, Work study, Cost benefit analysis, Performance measurement, Library effectiveness.

Information Technology and Information Systems and Programmes

26. Computer	Fundamentals, Hardware, Software, Humanware, application for House-keeping operations and services.
27. Information Technology	Concept, need and purpose, role in information transfer.
28. National and International Systems & Programming	INSDOC, NASSDOC, DESIDOC, SENDOC, UNESCO, IFLA, FID, UNISIST

29. National and International Networks	NISSAT, NICNET, INDONET, INFLIBNET, EURONET, BLAISE, OCLC, RLIN, AGRIS, INIS, DEVSIS, MEDLARS
30. Current Developments	Trends and research.

Research and Statistical Methods

31. Research	Need, purpose, levels, hypothesis and types
32. Research Design	
33. Tools and Techniques	Quantitative, qualitative, users and limitations
34. Methods of Research	Historical, Scientific, Descriptive, Comparative, Case Studies, Statistical

SAMPLE QUESTIONS

PAPER -II

1. An entry that directs the reader from one heading to another is called:

   (A) Added entry
   (B) Main entry
   (C) Analytical entry
   (D) Reference entry

[Key : (D)]

In the above "D" is the correct answer.

2. Who are the publishers of "Encyclopaedia of Library and Information Science"?:

   (A) American Library Association
   (B) H.W. Wilson
   (C) Marcel Dekker
   (D) R.R. Bowleer

[Key : (C)]

PAPER - III

1. Examine the usefulness of Translation Services in the multilingual country like India.
2. What do you understand by Scientific Management? How it can be applied to the management of a library?

ANNEXURE 5.4

Objectives of INFLIBNET

INFLIBNET is to be a computer-communication network for linking libraries and information centres in universities, deemed universities, institutions of national importance, UGC information centres, R&D institutions and colleges. The main objectives of INFLIBNET are:

(a) to evolve a national network, interconnecting various libraries and information centres in the country and to improve capability in information handling and service;

(b) to provide reliable access to document collection of libraries by creating online union catalogue of monographs, serials and non-book materials (manuscripts, audio-visuals, computer media, etc.) in various libraries in India;

(c) to provide better access to worthwhile bibliographic information sources, with citations and abstracts, such as periodical articles, conference papers, preprints, technical reports, standards and specifications, patents, monographs, etc. through indigenously created databases of the Sectoral Information Centres of NISSAT and UGC Information Centres and such others and by establishing gateways for online accessing of international databases held by international information networks and centres;

(d) to provide document delivery service by establishing resource centres around libraries having a rich collection of documents;

(e) to optimise information resource utilization through, shared cataloguing, inter-library loan service, catalogue production, collection development and avoiding duplication in acquisition to the extent possible;

(f) to implement computerisation of operations and services in the libraries and information centres of the country, following a uniform standard;

(g) to facilitate scientific communication amongst scientists, engineers, researchers, social scientists, academics, faculties and students through electronic mail, bulletin board, file transfer, computer/audio/video conferencing, etc;

(h) to enable the users disbursed all over the country, irrespective of location and distance, to have access to information regarding books, monographs, serials and non-book materials by locating the sources whereform available and to obtain it through the facilities of new communication technologies and union catalogue of documents;

(i) to create database of projects, institutions and specialists for providing online information service;

(j) to encourage co-operation among libraries, documentation centres and information centres in the country, so that the resources can be pooled for the benefit of helping the weaker resource centres by stronger ones.

ANNEXURE 5.5

Summary of Recommendations of Carl M. White Reports

The pace of library development in recent years has been rapid, but it has been outstripped by changes in the University which have transformed it into a major centre of advanced instruction and research. To catch up, the book collections have to be further strengthened, and more money will be required to do it. This however, is only the more obvious side of the matter. A great university library cannot be bought. It has to be built. The standards for building wisely and well involve standards of material support and standards of human support—library government, organization and administration, library personnel and service. Close examination of library conditions at the University of Delhi in the light of these standards shows that the entire structure of support needs strengthening. This calls for balanced effort which begins with action on fundamental library policy and organization and with improving the professional capabilities of the staff.

The object of the report is to assemble and organize information to be used by the several Departments and by other University authorities in analysing for themselves the library problem as it now stands. The heart of the report is the presentation of this information, chapter by chapter. From the labour of digging out this information and digging into its meaning, certain recommendations have emerged. In the aggregate they constitute a rounded programme of action which is contributed as a further aid toward completion of the task of self-analysis to which the University has set itself. The recommendations are summarised here for quick reference after they have been read in context first.

Chapter I—The University Library in Perspective

Recommendation: Base the case for library development on the premise that library service of high quality is the heart of an academic programme of high quality and complete the breakaway from the tradition inherited by the University that a library is a conventional but more or less useless accessory.

Recommendation: Get ready for increased per capita use. Current academic trends and improved services are sure to bring it and at the moment the library is not ready for it.

Chapter II —Conditions Favourable to Success

Recommendation: The University of Delhi has incurred special responsibilities for reasons of origin and location. If India is to give her full measure of support to the University, the facts about its history and success in meeting these responsibilities should be more widely known to the general public.

Recommendation: That the University undertakes to develop a library programme that is attuned both to its educational and broad social responsibilities.

Recommendation: No definitive set of standards for use in developing a university library programme exists, but hundreds of man years have been invested in crystallising those which are commonly agreed, in library literature, to be among the most essential. It is recommended that the university considers the applicability of such standards in dealing with local library problems.

Chapter III—The Book Collections

Recommendation: That book selection be oriented toward supporting instruction and research.

Recommendation: That the University uses the library to achieve the following results:

- To provide the resources necessary for research in fields of special interest to the University.
- To To aid the University teacher in keeping abreast of developments in his field.
- To provide the library facilities and services necessary for the success of all formal programmes of instruction.
- To open the door to the wide world of books that lie beyond the borders of one's own field of specialization.
- To bring books and people together under conditions which encourage reading for pleasure, self-discovery, personal growth and the sharpening of intellectual curiosity.

Recommendation: That the University adopt the practice of examining, with the aid of the Librarian, the library implications of a proposed educational programme as one of the steps necessary for determining whether the proposal is to be approved. When this is not done, the library programme and formal educational commitments are too loosely related to one another.

Recommendation: That the library undertake, as its part of coordinating library and educational policy, sympathetically to serve all educational programmes approved in accordance with the foregoing recommendation.

Recommendation: That expansion of the academic programme be correlated with the Library's capabilities in manpower, books and space to meet its share of all educational commitments.

Recommendation: That the University and the University Grants Commission examine the practical significance of long range library support and seek to provide support which is both stable and adequate in accordance with procedures which are mutually acceptable.

Recommendation: That the teaching staff and library staff work closely together to discard obsolete books and to determine in advance what titles are to be used intensively enough to require the purchase of additional copies.

Recommendation: That a special library fund be created for use in financing duplication of titles when it is adjudged to be necessary to provide adequate library support for the academic activities of the University.

Recommendation: That the Library Committee, in co-operation with Faculties and the Academic Council, study ways in which the guidance given to students in syllabi can be related more closely: (1) to Faculty co-operation in books selection, and (2) to the Library's efforts to cooperate in supporting the work of all teachers.

Recommendation: That the University's book-selection policy be broadened to include, as one objective, the development of a suitable collection of bibliographies and other important compilations of information which fall in the category of reference books.

Recommendation: That provision for regular purchase of reference books be made by annual allocation of funds for this purpose.

Recommendation: That while the University will wish to emphasize quality rather than the size in building its collection of journals, it is now receiving less than half the number which scholars consider necessary for their work. All journals which are essential for instruction and research should be obtained and the library should, if funds permit, accept responsibility shared by all major research libraries of obtaining, in addition to bare local necessities, other desirable journals as a contribution toward a rounded collection of research material for India as a whole.

Recommendation: That while the book stock has been, and is being rapidly developed, especially in some fields, the quality of the collections is uneven and the overall strength should be improved as the work of individual departments, which are themselves in development, requires it.

Recommendation: That the year 1965-66 be used to prepare basic lists of desiderata for purchase, the object being to relate book selection and purchase methodically to first priorities in instruction and research.

Recommendation: That in setting priorities for augmenting library resources, the University should give due attention to work of quality which is already well organized.

Recommendation: That the University study, in cooperation with such outside agencies as it deems appropriate, the implications of the findings reported in this chapter and related sections of other chapters—namely, that in making commitments in specific fields to develop instruction and research, problems of organizing the programme itself are receiving attention to the neglect of problems of planning the logistic of library support. Adequate library support for a programme cannot be improvised out of nothing. The answer is more careful planning, further ahead, and the University cannot solve the problems alone.

Recommendation: That the University of Delhi Library in cooperation with other libraries and appropriate departments within the University, pursue a more aggressive policy in collecting source material which should form part of the permanent literary, cultural and social record of India.

Recommendation: That the University join in stimulating nationwide interest in measures to ensure proper conservation and use of irreplaceable materials which are part of India's heritage.

Recommendation: That the University enlist the cooperation of its friends in obtaining a larger number of manuscripts and rare books either by purchase, photographic reproduction, or deposit.

Recommendation: That the University assist in the preservation and use of available special collections by arranging for them to be placed on deposit with the Library under terms mutually acceptable to the owner and to the University. Suitable accommodations should attract important collections, legal title to which should in due course pass to the University. It is in the nation's interest to help encourage the transfer of valuable private collections to a university where they can for all time serve the common good.

Recommendation: That in rounding out the books selection policy in accordance with the community's interest, account be taken of India's—and Delhi's—relation to the Commonwealth and to the English-speaking world in general.

Recommendation: That the University utilize the advice of the Librarian and the Department of History in developing an Oral History Project. The object is to produce through the use of well thought out and recorded interviews, source material of permanent significance for Indian history. It will be necessary, for security and to obtain cooperation, to guarantee that these recorded memories will be kept under seal and remain secret for as many years as the person desires.

Recommendation: That the Library Committee include on its agenda discussion with the Registrar, the Director of the University Press and others who are concerned, arrangements for permanent preservation and the use of archives of the University.

Chapter IV—The Government of the Library

Recommendation: That the Statutes and Ordinances be revised to provide an orderly basis for governing the library affairs of the University, the revision to embrace as a minimum the following objects:

1. Identify the type of material–books, periodicals and related graphic records—which is acquired for the permanent use of the University and draw a meaningful distinction between material of this sort on one hand and, on the other, permanent equipment of Departments of study and such material of a temporary, expendable nature as office supplies and dictionaries.

2. Assert University ownership of all books, periodicals, maps, pamphlets, slides, films, film-strips, etc., which are purchased or which are obtained by gift and exchange, for such permanent use and treat all these as legally a part of the library resources which are to be preserved for the common good.
3. Define the University Library (or libraries if the term is preferred) as the Authority which has legal title to all materials in this category.
4. Establish bibliographical control over these materials wherever they may be temporarily or permanently located. This means taking steps: (1) to organize all these materials so they can be easily and efficiently used, (2) to house and preserve them under suitable conditions, and (3) to maintain at all times suitable records of their whereabouts.
5. Use these materials and necessary staff to create library services of high standard. In creating geographically separate libraries, reconcile as justly as possible the conflicting claims of convenience on one hand and avoidable duplication of facilities and staff on the other. Doing so stretch money to buy a wider range of books.
6. Treat all these facilities, services and staff as comprising, regardless of physical location, a single library system and delegate responsibility for administering the system to a properly qualified librarian.
7. Encourage the University community and the head librarian to work together closely in maintaining and improving these services. As a two-way channel of communication to facilitate smooth, efficient service for all Departments and their students, make use of an advisory committee of Professor and Readers who are interested in, and equipped to facilitate, achieving fruitful results through active cooperation with the Librarian and his staff.

Recommendation: That the legal powers and responsibilities of the Librarian be defined, especially as they relate to the organization, support and operation of library services in the University.

Recommendation: That the post of Librarian be formally accorded high academic rank in keeping with the importance which libraries have assumed in the academic life of the University.

Recommendation: That the powers of management vested in the

Library Committee be formally delegated to the Librarian.

Recommendation: That the Librarian be answerable directly to the Vice-Chancellor for the performance of his duties.

Recommendation: That when the Library Committee and the University agree that it is time to discontinue the Committee-type of Library control now sanctioned by the Statutes and Ordinances, a Committee with advisory powers be created in accordance with terms acceptable to the Vice-Chancellor.

Recommendation: That the new Library Committee be excused from responsibility for staff appointments and that this responsibility be entrusted to Selection Committees in accordance with procedures followed in other academic departments.

Recommendation: That the legislative function pertaining to library regulations which is now divided between the Library Committee and the Academic Council be left to the Council, all such legislative proposals to originate with the Librarian and to be supported by the Library Advisory Committee.

Recommendation: That the Librarian may address a written report to the Vice-Chancellor each year summarising the activities and achievements of the library under his management. This report should be circulated for the information of the University and other interested citizens of India.

Recommendation: That the Librarian be charged with the duty of preparing estimates for the support of the library programme, details of procedure for approving these Estimates to be determined by the Vice-Chancellor.

Recommendation: That as a means of establishing confidence redefinition of the Library Committee's functions as advisory will not militate against effective library management any person who accepts responsibility for directing the libraries of the University of Delhi shali be accorded grade and academic rank which will assure him permanent security in accordance with the regular standards of tenure maintained by the University, but appointment to the chief post itself, by whatever title called, will be made on a term basis, renewable by mutual consent.

Recommendation: That the modification of terms governing appointment and tenure as described in the foregoing recommendation take effect when the next appointment is made and shall not affect terms governing the appointment of the present Librarian.

Recommendation: That the University encourage and support adoption of the policy of centralizing responsibility for the administration of all libraries maintained at University expense in the hands of the University Librarian.

Recommendation: That the timing of action on this recommendation take into account the desirability of making preparations far enough ahead to provide any Department affected by the change assurance that its interests and needs are to be adequately safeguarded.

Recommendation: That legal advice be sought to determine whether the University in fact hold to the Ratan Tata Library, especially that part of the collection which was acquired by the Delhi School of Economics prior to 20 December, 1957.

Chapter V—Library Administration

Recommendation: That the University can call attention of the University Grants Commission to the weakness inherent in the present policy of financing the University library and cooperate with the Commission in establishing provision for stable library financing at a level which will provide a basis for healthy development. Healthy growth of a library is more like child development than—say—physical plant development : it suffers from alternating years of plenty and years of famine. It is better to level out support from year to year.

Recommendation: That the University may draw attention to the fact that highly qualified manpower is as crucial to the success of a library programme as it is to the success of other academic programmes and that, to date, the method of financing the University Library fails to take this point adequately into account.

Recommendation: That since staff development has hitherto been heavily influenced by custodial and circulating-library functions, provision be made at an early date for additions to the staff with the degree of professional maturity necessary to reinforce present efforts of the staff to meet the service requirements of a research library clientele.

Recommendation: That as the work and organization of the Library gain stability, staff development be accepted as a function of good library administration and supervision; and that in the period immediately ahead in-service training be used as an aid to growth and efficiency in the performance or regular duties.

Recommendation: That as an aid to the Librarian and other ranking members of the Library staff in top-level supervision of staff and service, not less than 3 additional positions be created of the rank of Professional Senior or Librarian, the number to be decided in the light of action taken on recommendations in the report as a whole.

Recommendation: That the University define the standards by which its practice in the maintenance of Departmental libraries is to be guided.

Recommendation: That the decision on standards for maintaining Departmental libraries be made within a broader context—a long-range plan for decentralizing library services which takes due account of such factors as the economics of library service, the greatest convenience of the greatest number, and the bearing of larger units on a library's capabilities of providing services of a high order.

Recommendation: That a consultant on library building be retained to make a special analysis of how to relate present use of space to long-range building plans.

Recommendation: That a Science Library be created to serve the Departments which constitute the Faculty of Science; that the collection now maintained by these Departments and related material in the Main Library be used to form the nucleus of the new Library; that a Science Librarian of outstanding ability be employed to take charge of it; and that a new building be erected to house the Library.

Recommendation: That steps be taken as soon as practicable to create within the Main Library a more effective workshop for the scholars and advanced students in the Humanities.

Recommendation: That the policy of limiting the scope of Ratan Tata Library to economics be continued.

Recommendation: That the remaining social sciences be housed near the Main Library and that the services and space assignment in that building be adapted to the requirements of the Faculty of the Social Sciences as rapidly as possible.

Recommendation: That the administrative organization of the libraries be revised to provide a more effective basis for managing the library programme of the University.

Chapter VI—Services of the Library

Recommendation: That the Librarian and Heads of Departments of study cooperate in improving the organization of book selection.

Recommendation: That the Head of each Department personally, or some member of the Department designated by him, may serve as the channel for communicating to the Librarian, Departmental recommendations for book purchases. Whether the Department creates a Book Selection Committee or relies on some other method of evolving lists of books for purchase is an internal matter which can be decided by the Department itself.

Recommendation: That the library strengthen its present collection of aids to book selection and discuss with Departmental representatives how these aids can be consulted regularly and conveniently by all concerned.

Recommendation: That in determining whether to approve a research project, Department of study include, as part of their regular procedure, the examination and where necessary the strengthening of library resources to support the work.

Recommendation: That Departments of study be acquainted with adverse effects allowing requests for book purchases to pile up and that mutually satisfactory arrangements be worked out for a steadier flow of these requests to the library.

Recommendation: That responsibility for gifts and exchange be centralised and that this work be expanded both as a means of strengthening resources and conserving foreign exchange.

Recommendation: That the work-load of the Order Section be reduced by simplification of present procedures.

Recommendation: That all funds for library binding be transferred to the budget of the Library and that selection of a bindery or binderies be entrusted to the Librarian.

Recommendation: That the Library's success in adapting the classification of books to the needs of the local clientele as well as its success in facilitating access to these books through public catalogues be reviewed in the light of readers' experience in the use of the library.

Recommendation: That in preparation for stabilising and expanding the regular staff, the scope of the Processing Section's responsibilities be defined and a manning table worked out which shows the duties of each position and its relationship to other positions.

Recommendation: That high priority be given to developing the central catalogue into a union catalogue which records and shows the location of all books, journals and other materials in the various libraries of the University.

Recommendation: That use be made of tables, illustrations, posters, a suitable handbook and group instructions to diffuse knowledge of how the books are classified and how the public catalogues can be advantageously used.

Recommendation: That preparations for further staffing of the library, and particularly the Processing Section, as it is now called, take account of the fact that, during this study, Professors and Readers have indicated need of material in 11 modern and 4 ancient Indian languages as well as several foreign languages.

Recommendation: That reference service be strengthened and that miscellaneous duties now performed by the Reference Section which are not connected either with giving readers personal assistance in the use of the library or with the development of the book collections or with the development for publication to needed bibliographical tools, be assigned to Sections which can more appropriately handle them.

Recommendation: That consideration be given to limits of responsibility to be assumed by the Library for the success of a research project undertaken without first determining whether suitable library resources are available to support the project.

Recommendation: That the use and limitations of inter-library loans be more widely publicised.

Recommendation: That analysis be made of the feasibility of reducing the present failures to gain access to books from the general collection by identifying the type of material sought and determining whether access would be broadened by restricting normal use to library premises.

Recommendation: That in view of the size of the clientele consideration be given to promoting the usefulness of library resources by limiting a larger proportion of the more heavily used materials, books and periodicals, to *Reference Use;* and that, except for materials under special pressure, these materials be placed on open shelves, properly supervised to keep shelves in order and to provide reliable knowledge of their whereabouts.

Recommendation: That a system of issuing books be installed which will be speedier, simpler and more efficient for handling the volume of material now circulated by the Library.

Recommendation: That the University seek to base the rule of law governing the use of the library on a code of good citizenship which is enforceable but relieves the library of ultimate responsibility for enforcement.

Recommendation: That the library be regarded as an integral part of the University to which separate membership is not required; that formal membership in the University, however certified, and privileges of the University libraries.

Recommendation: That the University seek to achieve the following results without sacrificing its traditional goals of personal responsibility for public property, equal access, respect for one another's interests and enforcement of the rule of law:

(1) furtherance of the effectiveness and the pursuit of happiness of University Professors and Readers by lending materials for a period of unspecified duration, with the understanding that the material is always on call for another reader and will be promptly released on call from the Librarian or his representative;
(2) abolition of faculty overdue charges;
(3) permission of a student to read in the library, or to borrow, a book on any subject he pleases; and
(4) abolition of a special library fee.

Chapter VII—Financial Administration

Recommendation: That as an aid to efficient administration accounting procedure be approved to show plainly and accurately the total costs of operating the libraries which are maintained at University expense.

Recommendation: That in moving away from over-dependence on a succession of development grants, the University may adopt a functional approach to library development which hinges financial support on more systematic calculation of the resources (manpower, books, space) required to achieve programme objectives.

Recommendation: That while the University is building an integrated library programme of scope and strength sufficient to meet the requirements of the educational programme, the ratio of library expenditures to total educational expenditures be raised, if necessary, to a level higher than the average for most universities with a well-established tradition of stable support.

Recommendation: That the sum of Rs. 94,50,000 be used as a working estimate of the cost of non-current books and journals, manuscripts, maps and related sources required to build the books collection up to the point where, with suitable current additions, the present programme of instruction and research will have the library resources it requires.

Recommendation: That this outside estimate be reviewed as work on lists of desiderata progress in 1965-66.

Recommendation: That the addition of 27,500 volumes a year be used as an immediate objective in developing the acquisitions programme and that a stable book fund of Rs. 8,25,000 a year for the support of all Departments be sought for this purpose.

Recommendation: That as soon as future library policy for the University is developed to the point where it is fitting to do so, the Librarian be invited to revise tentative estimates for 1965-66 and the Fourth Five Year Plan.

Recommendation: That if programme objectives suggested in this report are approved, estimates may include provisions for nine additional librarians:

3 of the rank of Professional Senior or Librarian to help provide manpower of the quality necessary to fill administrative positions which the proposed reorganization of the University Library system would create.

1 of the rank of Professional Senior to serve as Science Librarian.

5 additional librarians of the rank of Professional Senior.

Recommendation: That the organization of the book budget provide for allocating each year separate funds under each of the following headings: (1) general works, including books of borderline interest; (2) Reference books; (3) Standing subscriptions; (4) Special materials for research; back files, expensive sets or other special purchases; and (5) subject funds to meet the basic needs of each recognised Department as at present.

Chapter VIII—Library Cooperation

Recommendation: That the present study of the libraries maintained at

University expense be supplemented by a study of the libraries of the constituent and affiliated colleges of the University.

Recommendation: That an object of the study be to determine how the colleges and the University can best work together to provide for all members of the academic community good library service at reasonable cost.

Recommendation: That consideration be given to coordinated administration of the college and the University libraries.

Recommendation: That Principals of the colleges join the University in considering the benefits to be derived from a centrally located library specially designed for undergraduate students.

Recommendation: That the University note the interdependence of the libraries of the city and the nation and note also be potential values of national library organization and leadership in helping improve local university library service.

Recommendation: That the Honourable Minister of Education be invited, through the University Grants Commission to consider the responsibility that devolves upon the Central Government for providing national aid and leadership in the development of library service as a significant social service for sustaining the intellectual and cultural independence of India.

Recommendation: That, subject to concurrence in the desirability of further attending to this responsibility, the Honourable Minister invite some professional organizations of international reputation, such as the American Library Association, to go into these recommendations more thoroughly.

ANNEXURE 5.6

Mehrotra Committee Recommendations to Improve Quality of Library Services

Importance of Libraries

The Library performs a crucial role in the educational process. It expands and supplements curricular learning. It widens the horizon. What is more important, the library even as it satisfies the quest for learning, spurs it to greater efforts. While passing on to the youthful generation the distilled wisdom of the human mind as it has evolved over the ages, the library sharpens the mind and clarifies concepts. It is the more durable bridge across time. The easiest way to assess the climate, temper and academic achievements of an educational institution is to visit its library and see how it is being maintained and utilised.

The importance of the library's role in imparting and disseminating knowledge has, of late, been enhanced by developments in continuing education, distance education and the open university systems. The introduction and expansion of a nation-wide scheme of these systems is essential for a country which faces a huge backlog of illiteracy and which nevertheless is keen to embark on the 21st Century in the company of the educationally and scientifically most advanced nations of the world. The University/College libraries assume an even greater importance in a country like India where the majority of students cannot purchase any, but the most essential books.

The vital significance of the libraries in the educational system has been voiced by various Commissions, including the Education Commission (1964–66). Without a good library, high quality instruction and research in colleges and universities would be entirely inconceivable. The Committee is, however, constrained to remark that despite the recognition of a library's importance, the functioning of the libraries has not undergone any radical improvement. In many of the colleges, the library is neither adequately housed; nor properly laid out. Some of these are not sufficiently lit; nor properly ventilated. There is no system of display of recent additions to the library. There is no serious efforts to facilitate location and retrieval of books and journals. Consequently, the seeker has to fend for himself. Some of these traits are applicable to the university libraries as well. A library should be so housed, laid out, equipped and manned as to attract the students and teachers and to generate in them an urge to delve into latest thinking no subjects in which they are interested. A good library not only stores but radiates knowledge.

It is in this context that the Education Policy (1986) envisages provision of library facilities in all educational institution and improvement in the status of librarians.

Functions of a Librarian

A Librarian is expected to provide a wide range of services to the user. He is required to make available in a convenient and attractive form to students and faculty members, a well-organised and properly arranged stock of books, journals and other relevant material which is to be kept properly indexed, catalogued and up-dated. The librarian has to provide reading and lending facilities and services relating to reference and bibliography, extension, documentation and reprography. It should be his constant endeavour to widen and update his range of knowledge so that he can extend valuable guidance to teachers as well as students.

Because of the rapid expansion of knowledge which is assessed to be doubling itself every seven years, and a continuous flow of data and information, the use in libraries of modern technological innovation has become inevitable. The librarian, therefore, has to be fully conversant with the modern techniques of library management. It is undeniable that a librarian, although he is not a formal member of the teaching faculty, performs academic functions, and sustains and enriches the academic process. While a teacher may have specialised in a particular branch, the librarian is required to have a wide overall acquaintance with various disciplines in order to be able to bring the scholars face to face with knowledge in diverse areas. The students, contact with the librarian should be exhilarating and educative. The Librarian's interaction with members of the faculty should be of mutual benefit. It is expected that the accession of latest books and journals, the queries of students and interaction with teachers would keep the librarian mentally alert and sufficiently knowledgeable. Evidently, he must be qualified and trained for the purpose. It follows that the emoluments of the duly qualified librarians should match those of the teachers and that they should have about the same promotional opportunities as have been recommended for the teachers.

The librarians in colleges and universities should be provided adequate facilities to enable them to improve their qualifications and bring them to the level of the desired standards. The universities that have departments of library and Information Science should draw up appropriate courses for summer schools. These courses should be specially designed to impart education about modern technological developments in the field of library science. The purpose shall be to improve services to the students and faculty members.

In Part-A of the report, the Committee has dealt at length with the qualifications for recruitment of teachers in colleges and universities. In order to draw upon a wider range of talent, the Committee did not lay down M.Phil/Ph.D. as an essential qualification for recruitment. Recognising, however, the importance of exposure to research as an important input for teaching, the Committee did recommend higher salary for candidates recruited with M.Phil/Ph.D. degrees. For those recruited without these, the Committee recommended the provision of adequate in-service facilities. It further suggested a national qualifying test for eligibility. The Committee recommends a similar eligibility test for Librarianship at the initial stage of recruitment. Librarians will be recruited out of those who have passed the eligibility test. This would facilitate the work of selection committees, even without the effect of disparities in standards of marking, and improve the quality of entrants.

In order to base career prospects on merit, competence and ability, it is essential to introduce a system of assessment for the librarians. As in the case of teachers, this assessment should consist of a combination of self-assessment and external assessment. It is suggested that every librarian should be asked to prepare a self-assessment report at the end of each academic session. This report should include items like number of days the library was kept open, daily average of readers, average number of books issued, new acquisitions, book exhibition, if any, additions to data bank, documentation, introduction of new techniques/procedures to improve service to the users, participation in conferences, seminars, refresher courses, workshops etc., list of publications, documentation/bibliography abstraction and reviews. The improvements effected and the facilities and guidance provided should, in particular, be highlighted.

In addition to self-assessment, assessment by users should constitute an important index to the Librarian's performance. A method should be devised whereby faculty and students are asked about the quality of library services made available to them. Some of the suggestions given by the users can, in fact, form the basis for improvement in library services. Besides self-assessment and assessment by users, the work of the librarian should also be annually reviewed by the Principal in a College and Dean or Vice-Chancellor in a University. Good performance as reflected in the assessment will constitute the basis for further promotion, which will be performance-bound. the Librarian should be equipped and disposed to innovate and to introduce modern techniques. He should also strive to bring about improvements within the existing facilities.

The promotion of librarians should be linked with the acquisition of additional qualifications. In the context of the rapid developments in modern technology in management of libraries, it becomes essential that librarians be given opportunities, like duty leave etc., for improving their competence. They should also be enabled to attend summer schools, workshops and seminars and satisfactory performance in these summer schools may be taken into account for promotion. While the progress in information science and technology demands a substantial increase in the technical competence of librarians, their academic (i.e. subject) competence and general awareness have also to be upgraded continuously.

The Committee has suggested three thrust areas for the Librarians:

1. Training in modern library technology.
2. General awareness and acquaintance with the gamut of disciplines.
3. Making visit to the library an exciting and elevating experience.

The preceding suggestions would make it necessary to restructure and reinforce B.Lib. and M.Lib. courses.

In Universities, where there is a network of departmental libraries, the Central Library should not function in isolation as some-times the departmental libraries do not receive adequate attention from the University Librarian. Often the staff posted to the departmental libraries lacks both supervisory control and promotion prospects. The Committee would, therefore, recommend that the staff of the departmental libraries should invariably be on the pooled cadre and under the administrative control of the Central Library. The University Librarian and his Deputies should be responsible for overseeing or running on periodical basis functioning of these departmental libraries.

ANNEXURE 5.7

Revision of Pay Scales — Document No. F.1-21/87-U.1 Dated 22nd July, 1988

Subject: Revision of pay scales of teachers in Universities and Colleges and other measures for maintenance of standards in Higher Education.

Sir,

I am directed to say that vide this Department's letter of even number dated June 17, 1987, the decisions of the Government of India on the revision of pay scales of teachers in universities and colleges with effect from January 1, 1986 and provision of financial assistance to the State Governments to adopt and implement the scheme, were communicated to all State Governments and Union Territories. Subsequently, this department had vide Education Secretary's D.O. letter of even number dated September 7, 1987, addressed to Education Secretaries of all the State Governments, communicated certain modifications/clarifications relating to some of the provisions of the scheme announced on June 17, 1987. However, in the letter of September 7, 1987, there was no mention of the selection grade for Lecturers; it was mentioned that the revision of pay scales of Librarians and Physical Education Personnel was under consideration.

2. The Government have since considered all these matters. It has been decided to make the following amendments to the scheme appended to this Ministry's letter of even number dated June 17, 1987:

Scales of Pay

(i) The two scales of pay of Readers mentioned in Annexure I to the Scheme are combined into a single scale of Rs. 3700-125-4950-150-5700. Consequently all existing Readers and Selection Grade Lecturers in Colleges in the scale of Rs. 1200-1900 will be placed in the revised scale of Rs. 3700-5700. The revised Selection

Grade for Lecturers will also be Rs. 3700-5700.

(ii) The revised pay of the Vice-Chancellor will be Rs. 7600 (fixed). This revised pay is applicable to Central Universities. The State Governments may, if they so wish, adopt this pay for State Universities also. But no financial assistance will be available from the Central Government for this purpose.

(iii) The Scheme of Professor of Eminence is being further examined and a decision in this regard will be communicated in due course.

(iv) Para 10 of the Scheme together with its explanation is deleted. Instead, the following provision is added:

> "In order to encourage research, in continuation of Post-graduate studies, candidates who, at the time of recruitment as lecturers, possess Ph.D. or M.Phil. degree (hereinafter called jointly as the "research degree"), will be sanctioned three and one advance increments respectively in the scale of Rs. 2200-4000 alongwith the benefit of the corresponding years of service for the purpose of promotion. The existing Lecturers without research degrees and those similarly situate recruited in future will be eligible for a similar benefit in service for the purpose of promotion as and when they acquire research degrees, but will not be eligible for advance increments. Existing Lecturers with research degrees will also be eligible for a similar benefit.

(v) Consequently, explanations (i) and (ii) below para 8 of the Scheme are also deleted.

Career Advancement

(vi) Sub-clause (b) of para 11 of the Scheme which provides for possession of M.Phil. or Ph.D. degree to become eligible for placement in the Senior Scale is deleted. Participation in two refresher courses/summer institutes should each be of approximately four weeks, duration, and other appropriate continuing education programmes of comparable quality as may be specified by the University Grants Commission may also be accepted for this purpose.

(vii) Every Lecturer in the Senior Scale will be eligible for promotion to the post of Reader in the scale of Rs. 3700-5700 if he/she has:

(a) Completed 8 years of service in the senior scale, provided that the requirement of 8 years will be relaxed if the total service of the lecturer is not less then 16 years;

(b) obtained a Ph.D. degree, or an equivalent published work;

(c) made some mark in the areas of scholarship and research as evidenced by self-assessment, reports of referees, quality of publications, contribution to educational renovation, design of new courses and curricula, etc.;

(d) participated in two refresher courses/summer institutes each of approximately 4 weeks, duration, or engaged in other appropriate continuing education programmes of comparable quality as may be specified by the UGC after placement in the Senior Scale; and

(e) consistently good performance appraisal reports.

(viii) Promotion to the Post of Reader will be through a process of selection by a Selection Committee to be set up under the Statutes/Ordinances of the University concerned or other similar Committees set up by the appointing authorities in accordance with the guidelines to be laid down by the UGC.

(ix) Those Lecturers in the Senior Scale who do not have Ph.D. degree or equivalent published work and who do not meet the scholarship and research standards, but fulfil the other criteria prescribed for promotion to the post of Reader and have a good record in teaching and/or participation in extension activities, will be placed in the grade of Rs. 3700-5700, subject to the recommendations of the Selection Committee for promotion to the post of Reader. They will be designated as Lecturers in the Selection Grade. They could offer themselves for fresh assessment after obtaining Ph.D. and/or fulfilling other requirements for promotion as Readers, and if found suitable, could be given the designation of Reader.

(x) For placement of Lecturers in the Senior Scale and Selection Grade as well as for promotion to the post of Reader, the required number of positions would be created by upgrading the posts held by the incumbents concerned.

(xi) Promotions made under the Merit Promotion Scheme of the UGC, or any other similar schemes before the announcement of the revised scales on 17-6-1987 will not be re-opened. However, in such cases the benefit of revision will be available to teachers only from the date of their promotion.

3. For facility of reference, the scheme incorporating all the amendments and also such changes as are consequential or incidental to the amendments is attached to this letter as Appendix-I.
4. The revised pay scales of Librarians and Physical Education Personnel are the same as are approved for teachers. The revised scales will be admissible only to those Librarians and Physical Education Personnel who have been sanctioned the scales of pay of Lecturers, Readers and Professors under the 1973 revision namely, Rs. 700-1600, Rs. 1200-1900 and Rs. 1500-2500. The cases of existing Librarians and Physical Education Personnel who are on scales of pay lower than Rs. 700-1600 will be considered separately after making an assessment of their existing scales of pay, the qualifications and other relevant factors obtaining in various States. The revised scales of pay now approved are not therefore, admissible on the basis of designations alone; they have to be sanctioned keeping also in view the existing scales of pay. Since the qualifications, method of recruitment and criteria for career advancement are slightly different in the case of Librarians and Physical Education Personnel, in the light of the requirements of their profession, the relevant provisions of the scheme as far as they relate to these matters are marginally different from those applicable to teachers. The revised pay scales and the relevant conditions relating to recruitment, qualifications and career advancement approved by the Government for Librarians and Physical Education Personnel are given in Appendix II to the letter.
5. All other terms and conditions for revision of pay scales of Librarians and Physical Education Personnel are the same as indicated in Appendix-I to this letter. The terms and conditions for payment of Central assistance to the State Governments for the revision of pay scales of Librarians and Physical Education Personnel in the Universities and Colleges will be the same as those mentioned in this Department's letter of even number dated June 17, 1987.
6. Several State Governments have already issued orders regarding the implementation of the revision of pay scales of teachers. They are requested kindly to review the orders already issued by them

in the light of the amendments now made and incorporate appropriate changes in the orders issued by them. Such amendments may kindly be sent for consideration in this Department so that Central assistance to the extent admissible can be sanctioned.

7. The receipt of this letter may kindly be acknowledged.

Revised Pay Scales of Librarians in the Universities and Colleges from 1-1-1986

Designation	Existing Scales of Pay	Revised Scales of Pay
A. University		
1. Assistant Librarian/ Documentation Officer	700-1600	2200-75-2800-100-4000
2. Assistant Librarian/ Documentation Officer (Senior Scale)	Not Existing	3000-100-3500-125-5000
3. Assistant Librarian/ Documentation Officer (Selection Grade)	Not Existing	3700-125-4950-150-5700
4. Deputy Librarian	1200-1900	3700-125-4950-150-5700
5. Librarian	1500-2500	4500-150-5700-200-7300
B. Colleges		
1. College Librarian	700-1600	2200-75-2800-100-4000
2. College Librarian (Senior Scale)	Not Existing	3000-100-3500-125-5000
3. College Librarian (Selection Grade)	Not Existing	3700-125-4950-150-5700

Appendix II to Ministry of Human Resource Development (Department of Education) Letter No.F. 1-21/87-U.I dated the 22nd July, 1988 Regarding Revision of Pay Scales of Librarians and Physical Education Personnel in Universities and Colleges

Coverage

1. The revised pay scales mentioned hereinafter apply to all Universities and Colleges which are covered by the scheme of revision of pay scales of teachers mentioned in the Appendix to the Ministry of Human Resource Development (Deptt. of

Education), letter No. F.1-21/87-U.I. dated June 17, 1987.

Terms and Conditions

2. All the terms and conditions for revision of pay scales mentioned in the Appendix referred to in para I above shall apply to the revision of pay scales of Librarians and Physical Education Personnel in Universities and Colleges except to the extent indicated in the following paragraphs.

Pay Scales

3. The revised scales of pay effective from 1.1.1986 for Librarians and Physical Education Personnel are those mentioned in Annexures I and II of this Report respectively.

Recruitment and Qualifications

4. Recruitment to the posts of Assistant Librarian, Deputy Librarian as well as Assistant Director, Deputy Director and Director of Physical Education in the Universities shall be on the basis of merit through All-India advertisement and Selection, provided that Assistant Librarians and Assistant Directors of Physical Education who fulfil the criteria prescribed herein-after will be eligible for promotion to the posts of Deputy Librarian and Deputy Director of Physical Education respectively. Recruitment to the posts of Librarians and Director/Instructor of Physical Education in Colleges shall be on the basis of merit through All-India advertisement and selection.
5. The minimum qualifications required for appointment to the posts mentioned in para 4 above will be those prescribed by the UGC from time to time.
6. As in the case of recruitment of Lecturers in Universities and Colleges, only those candidates who, besides fulfilling the minimum academic qualifications prescribed for the post of Assistant Librarian/Assistant Director of Physical Education in Universities and Librarian and Director/Instructor of Physical Education in Colleges, have qualified in a comprehensive test will be eligible for appointment to these posts. The detailed scheme for conducting the test including its design, the agencies

to be employed for conducting the test, etc. will be worked out and communicated by the University Grants Commission.

7. Candidates who, at the time of their recruitment as Assistant Librarians and Assistant Directors of Physical Education in Universities, and Librarians and Directors/Instructors of Physical Education in Colleges, possess M.Phil, or Ph.D. Degrees in Library Science or Physical Education, as the case may be, will be sanctioned one and three advance increments respectively in the scale of Rs. 2200-4000 alongwith the benefit of corresponding years of service for the purpose of promotion. The existing incumbents without research degrees and those similarly situate recruited in future, will be eligible for a similar benefit in service for the purpose of promotion as and when they acquire research degrees, but will not be eligible for advance increments. Existing incumbents with research degrees will also be eligible for a similar benefit.

Career Advancement

8. Every Assistant Librarian and Assistant Director of Physical Education in a University and a Librarian and Director/Instructor of Physical Education in a college, who is in the scale of pay of Rs. 2200-4000 will be placed in a Senior Scale of Rs. 3000-5000 if he/she has:

(a) completed 8 years' service after regular appointment, with relaxation as provided in para 7 above;
(b) participated in two refresher courses/summer institutes, each of approximately four week's; duration or engaged in other appropriate continuing education programme of comparable quality as may be specified by the UGC; and
(c) consistently satisfactory performance appraisal reports.

Explanation

All existings incumbent of these posts in the Universities and Colleges, who are in the scale of pay of Rs. 700-1600 and who have completed 8 years of service on 1.1.1986, will be placed through a process of screening/selection as indicated in para 22 of Appendix I to this letter, in the scale of Rs. 3000-5000. The benefit of service provided in para 7 will be available for the initial placement also.

9. Every Assistant Librarian and Assistant Director of Physical Education in the Universities who has been placed in the Senior Scale will be eligible for promotion to the post of Deputy Librarian and Deputy Director of Physical Education respectively in the scale of pay of Rs. 3700-5700 if he/she has:

   (a) completed 8 years of service in the senior scale: provided that the requirement of 8 years will be relaxed if his/her total service is not less than 16 years;
   (b) obtained a Ph.D. degree or an equivalent published work;
   (c) made significant contributions to the development of Library Service/Physical Education in the University as evidenced by self-assessment reports of referees, professional improvement in the Library Services/Physical Education activities, etc., as the case may be;
   (d) participated in two refresher courses/summer institutes each of approximately 4 weeks' duration, or engaged in other appropriate continuing education programmes of comparable quality as may be specified by the UGC, after placement in the senior scale; and
   (e) consistently good in performance appraisal reports.

10. Promotion to the post of Deputy/Librarian Deputy Director of Physical Education will be through a process of selection by a Selection Committee as in the case of promotion to the posts of Readers. Posts of Deputy Librarians/Deputy Directors of Physical Education will be created for this purpose by upgrading the post of Assistant Librarian/Director of Physical Education (Senior Scale).
11. Those Assistant Librarians and Assistant Directors of Physical Education in the Universities in the Senior Scale who do not have Ph.D. degree or equivalent published work, but fulfil the other criteria, mentioned in para 9 above, will be placed in the grade of Rs. 3700-5700, subject to the recommendations of the Committee mentioned in para 10 above. They will be designated as Assistant Librarian and Assistant Director of Physical Education in the Selection Grade.
12. The College Librarians and Directors/Instructors of Physical

Education in Colleges, who have been placed in the Senior Scale will also be eligible for placement in the Selection Grade of Rs. 3700-5700 if they fulfil the criteria prescribed in para 11 above.

Anomalies

13. Anomalies, if any, in the implementation of the scheme may be brought to the notice of the Department of Education in the Ministry of Human Resource Development for clarification.

Appendix 1 to Ministry of Human Resource Development (Department of Education), letter No.F.1-21/87.U.I. dated July 22, 1988 regarding the Scheme of Revision of pay scales of Teachers in Universities and Colleges, 1986 and other Measures for Maintenance of Standards in High Education

Coverage

1. This Scheme applies to teachers in all Universities (excluding Agricultural Universities), and Colleges (excluding Agricultural, Medical and Veterinary Science Colleges) admitted to the privileges of the Universities unless they specifically exercise an option in writing to remain out of this Scheme as provided in para 19 hereafter. All teachers appointed after the date from which the scheme has been given effect will be governed by the provisions of the scheme.

Explanation

(i) The Scheme will apply to teachers in the Faculties of Agriculture, Medicine and Veterinary Sciences in the Central Universities.
(ii) The Scheme of revision of pay scales of teachers in technical institutions (including Engineering Colleges and other Institutions offering courses only in Technical Education) will be communicated separately.

Date of Effect

2. The revised scales of pay will be effective from January 1, 1986.

Pay Scales

3. The revised scales of pay effective from 1-1-1986.
4. The revised scales of pay are inclusive of the basic pay, the dearness pay, the dearness allowances, additional dearness allowance, and the interim relief, if any, admissible to teachers as on 1.1.1986.
5. The revised scale of pay of Tutors and Demonstrators is for the existing incumbents of these positions in the Universities and Colleges. There shall be no fresh recruitment to this category.
6. The Principals of Colleges may be placed in the scale of pay of Reader or Professor on the basis of criteria to be laid down by the State Governments.
7. The revised pay for Vice-Chancellors indicated in Annexure I of this report is applicable to Central Universities. The State Governments may, if they so wish, adopt this pay for State Universities also. But, no financial assistance will be available from the Central Government for this purpose.
8. The Scheme of Professors of Eminence is being further examined and a decision in this regard will be communicated in due course.

Recruitment and Qualifications

9. Recruitment to the posts of Lecturers, Readers and Professors in Universities and Colleges shall be on the basis of merit through All-India advertisement and selection, provided that Lecturers who fulfil the criteria prescribed in this scheme will be eligible for promotion to the posts of Readers.
10. The minimum qualifications required for appointment to the posts of Lecturers, Readers and Professors will be those prescribed by the UGC from time to time. Generally, the minimum qualifications for appointment to the post of Lecturer in the scale of pay of Rs. 2200-4000 shall be Master's degree in the relevant subject with at least 55 per cent marks or its equivalent grade, and good academic record.
11. Only those candidates who, besides fulfilling the minimum academic qualifications prescribed for the post of Lecturer, have qualified in a comprehensive test, to be specially conducted for the purpose, will be eligible for appointment as Lecturers. The detailed scheme for conducting the test including its design, the

agencies to be employed in the conduct of tests, content, administration, etc., will be worked out by the UGC, keeping in view the requirements of the media of instruction followed by the different States/Universities/Colleges, and other relevant considerations.

12. In order to encourage research, in continuation of Post-graduate studies, candidates who, at the time of their recruitment as Lecturers, possess Ph.D. or M.Phil degree-will be sanctioned three and one advance increments respectively in the scale of Rs. 2200-4000 alongwith the benefit of corresponding years of service for the purpose of promotion. The existing Lecturers without research degrees, and those similarly situate, recruited in future will eligible for a similar benefit in service for the purpose of promotion as and when they acquire research degree, but will not be eligible for advance increments. Existing Lecturers with research degrees will also be eligible for a similar benefit.

Career Advancement

13. Every Lecturers will be placed in a senior scale of Rs. 3000-5000 if he/she has:

(a) Completed 8 years of service after regular appointment, with relaxation as provided in para 12 above;
(b) Participated in two refresher courses/simmer institutes, each of approximately 4 weeks' duration or engaged in other appropriate continuing education programmes of comparable quality as may be specified by the UGC;
(c) consistently satisfactory performance appraisal reports.

Explanation
All Lecturers in the existing scale of Rs. 700-1600, who have completed 8 years of service on 1.1.1986, will be placed through a process of screening/selection as indicated in para 22 below in the scale of Rs. 3000-5000. The benefit of service provided in para 12 will be available for the initial placement also.

14. Every Lecturer in the Senior scale will be eligible for promotion to the post of Reader in the scale of pay of Rs. 3700-5700 if he/she has:

(a) completed 8 years of service in the Senior Scale, provided that the requirement of 8 years will be relaxed, if the total service of the Lecturer is not less than 16 years;
(b) obtained a Ph.D. degree, or an equivalent published work;
(c) made some mark in the areas of scholarship and research as evidenced by self-assessment, reports of referees, quality of publications, contribution to educational renovation, design of new courses and curricula, etc.;
(d) participated in two refresher courses/summer institutes each of approximately 4 weeks' duration or engaged in other appropriate continuing education programmes of comparable quality as may be specified by the UGC, after placement in the Senior Scale; and
(e) consistently good performance appraisal reports.

15. Promotion to the post of Reader will be through a process of selection by a Selection Committee to be set up under the Statutes/Ordinances of the University concerned or other similar Committees set up by the appointing authorities in accordance with the guidelines to be laid down by the UGC. Posts of Readers will be created for this purpose by upgrading a corresponding number of posts of Lecturers in the Universities and Colleges.
16. Those Lecturers in the Senior Scale who do not have Ph.D. Degree or equivalent published work and who do not meet the scholarship and research standards of a Reader, but fulfill the other criteria mentioned in para 14, and have a good record in teaching and/or participation in extension activities, will be placed in the grade of Rs. 3700-5700, subject to the recommendations of the Committee mentioned in para 15 above. They will be designated as Lecturer in the Selection Grade. Posts in the Selection Grade will be created for this purpose by upgrading the posts held by them. They could offer themselves for a fresh assessment after obtaining Ph.D. and or fulfilling other requirements for promotion as Reader, and if found suitable, could be given the designation of Reader.
17. Lecturers in the existing Selection Grade of Rs. 1200-1900 in the Colleges will be placed at the appropriate stage in the revised Selection Grade of Rs. 3700-5700 in accordance with the pay fixation formula under this scheme. Existing Lecturers, who have completed or will complete, a total period of sixteen years of

service on 1.1.1986 or thereafter will be eligible for promotion to the post of Reader or placement in the Selection Grade in accordance with the provision's in paras 14, 15 and 16. They will also be entitled to the relaxation in the years of service by 3 years and 1 year respectively if they hold Ph.D. or M.Phil. degrees as mentioned in para 12.

18. More posts of Professors and Readers will be created in the Universities and Colleges to broaden the channel of open selection. The UGC would evolve suitable criteria for this purpose. The requirements of qualifications and experience for posts to be filled up through open selection will be prescribed by the UGC from time to time. Universities will have the freedom to seek out brilliant people, independent of their seniority, from within the Universities and Colleges, or outside, and provide them opportunities for joining the teaching profession at appropriate levels.
19. The existing teachers in Universities and Colleges where the Merit Promotion Scheme formulated by the UGC in 1983, or any other similar schemes are in operation will have an option to continue to be governed by the provisions of those schemes' provided that they exercise that option in writing prior to their pay fixation under this scheme. They will also be entitled to the designations envisaged for various categories of teachers in those schemes, but the scales of pay will be as follows:

(i)	Lecturer	–	Rs. 2200-4000
(ii)	Reader/Lecturer (Selection Grade)	–	Rs. 3000-5000
(iii)	Professor	–	Rs. 4500-5700

20. The promotions made before the announcement of the revised scale on 17.6.1987, will not be reopened. However, in such cases, the benefit of revision will be available to teachers only from the date of their promotion.

Continuing Education and Appraisal of Performance

21. Participation of teachers at regular intervals in appropriate continuing education programmes is envisaged as an integral part of the professional development of teachers. The University

Grants Commission, the Indira Gandhi National Open University, the State Governments and other appropriate agencies will be advised to take steps to introduce programmes of continuing education for this purpose through a variety of means. While there cannot and need not be any rigid requirement of participation in formal programmes, evidence of commitment to continuing education of any recognised means, as may be specified by the UGC will be an essential requirement for career advancement. Pending the organisation of such programmes on the quality and scale required for giving effect to the implementation of the measures envisaged in paras 13 to 17 of this scheme, relaxation from the requirement of participation in such programmes for specific period and for specific categories of posts, will be granted by the University concerned in accordance with guidelines to be laid down by the UGC.

22. Regular and systematic appraisal of performance of teachers is to be an essential element in the management of education and this has been taken into account in the design for the career development of teachers. The UGC has been requested to formulate the guidelines for the evaluation of performance of teachers, taking into account the statement contained in the National Policy on Education, 1986. Such a system should become operational with effect from academic year 1988-89. Till it becomes operational the existing screening mechanism/selection procedures or those prescribed on a provisional basis by the University/State Government concerned will apply to all placements/promotions referred to in paras 13 to 17.

Other Conditions of Service

Probation

23. The period of probation of a teacher shall not exceed a period of 24 months. A lecturer appointed on probation should ordinarily be confirmed only after he/she has completed an appropriate short-term orientation programme and his/her performance appraisal reports are satisfactory. The UGC has been requested to take arrangements to ensure that facilities are available for organising orientation programmes to cover all lecturers

appointed in and after 1988-89.

Superannuation and re-employment

24. The age of superannuation for teachers should be 60 years and thereafter no extension in service should be given. However, it will be open to a University or College to re-employ a superannuated teacher according to the existing guidelines framed by the UGC, up to the age of 65 years.

Grievance Redressal Mechanism

25. Appropriate mechanism for the redressal of teachers' grievances will be established in all Universities and Colleges, in respect of which guidelines will be issued separately.

Code of Professional Ethics

26. The UGC will prepare a Code of Professional Ethics for teachers in consultation with the representatives of national level associations of teachers; all concerned should see to the observance of the Code.

Pay Fixation Formula

27. The pay of teachers in the revised scale on 1.1.1986 will be fixed in accordance with the formula recommended by the Fourth Pay Commission while revising pay scales of the Central Government employees. The details of the pay fixation formula are given in order under reference.

Dearness Allowance and other benefits

28. (a) The revised scale of pay on 1.1.1986 is inclusive of the dearness pay and dearness allowance admissible on that date. Any dearness allowance that might become due after that date will have to be sanctioned by the agencies which are meeting the maintenance expenditure of the concerned Universities and Colleges.
    (b) Teachers in the Central Universities and institutions financed

by the Central Government are sanctioned dearness allowance at the rate applicable to Central Government employees drawing corresponding pay. The are also sanctioned other benefits like House Rent Allowance, House Building Advance, medical facilities, pension and other retirement benefits, leave travel concession, group insurance, etc. on the pattern of similar benefits available to corresponding categories of Central Government employees. The State Government may consider providing comparable benefits in the light of the statement made in the National Policy on Education, 1986.

Anomalies

29. Anomalies, if any, in the implementation of the scheme may be brought to the notice of Department of Education in the Ministry of Human Resource Development for clarification.

ANNEXURE 5.8

Qualifications and Grades of Librarians – Document No. F. 1-9/89 (CPP-I) dated 20th February 1990

Subject: Minimum Qualification for the recruitment to the posts of Librarian, Deputy Librarian, Assistant Librarian, College Librarian and Documentation Officer in the Universities and Colleges.

Sir,

In supersession of this Office Circular No. F.1-96/81 (CP/MP) dated the 31st August, 1984 on the above subject, I am directed to enclose revised qualifications for recruitment to the posts of Librarian, Deputy Librarian, Assistant Librarian, College Librarian and Documentation Officer in the Universities and Colleges, consequent upon the revision of pay scales of teachers in the Universities and Colleges w.e.f. Ist January, 1986.

Minimum qualification for appointment to the posts of Librarian, Dy. Librarian, Assistant Librarian/College Librarian & Documentation Officer.

1. **Librarian : (University)** (Rs. 4500-150-5700-200-7300)

(i) Master's Degree in Library Science/Information Science/-Documentation with at least fifty-five per cent marks or its equivalent grade and a consistently good academic record;
(ii) One year specialisation in an area of information technology/ Archives and Manuscript keeping, Master's Degree in an area of thrust in the institution;
(iii) At least ten years as a Deputy Librarian in University Library or fifteen years experience as a college librarian; and
(iv) Evidence of innovative library service and organisation of published work.

Desirable:
M.Phil/Ph.D. degree in Library Science/Information Science Documentation/Archives and Manuscript keeping.

2. **Deputy Librarian** (Rs. 3700-125-4900-150-5700)

(i) Master's Degree in Library Science/Information Science/-Documentation with at least fiftyfive percent marks or its equivalent grade and a consistently good academic record;
(ii) One year specialisation in an area of information technology/-Archives and Manuscript keeping or Master's Degree in an area of thrust in the institution;
(iii) Eight year's experience as an Assistant University Librarian/-College Librarian; and
iv. Evidence of innovative library services, published work and professional commitment.

Desirable

M.Phil/Ph.D. degree in Library Science/Information Science/-Documentation/Archives and Manuscript keeping.

3. **Assistant University Librarian/College Librarian Documentation Officer**

(Rs.200-75-2800-100-4000)

(i) Qualifying the national level test conducted for the purpose by the UGC or any other agency approved by the UGC.
(ii) Master's Degree in Library Science/Information Science/ Documentation or an equivalent professional degree with atleast fiftyfive percent marks or its equivalent grade plus a consistently good academic record;

OR

Master's degree in Arts/Science/Commerce or equivalent degree with at least fifty-five per cent marks or its equivalent grade with Bachelor's degree in Library Science/Information Science/Documentation or an equivalent professional degree with atleast fiftyfive percent marks or its equivalent grade plus a consistently good academic record.

BIBLIOGRAPHY OF DOCUMENTS CITED

Committee on Colleges – Report, New Delhi, UGC, 1967.

Committee on Model Act for Universities – Report Ministry of Education, New Delhi, Government of India, 1964.

Development of Higher Education and research in the Universities 1980-85, New Delhi, UGC, 1986.

Education Commission (1964-66) – Report, Ministry of Education, New Delhi, Govt. of India, 1971.

Education for our people: A policy frame for the development of Education (1978-87), Bombay, Allied, 1978.

Education and values, by D.S. Kothari.

Eighth Plan perspectives on Journalism/communication education in India, New Delhi, UGC, 1990

Future Education and Human Resource, Management, Reddy, V.N.K., Delhi, Bhartiya, 1988.

Governance of Indian Universities Pt. I, New Delhi, UGC, 1971.

Guidelines for providing Assistance to Arts Science, Commerce and multi-faculty college for development during the Seventh plan period (1985-90), New Delhi, UGC, 1986.

Guidelines for formulating proposals for the eighth plan development schemes of Universities, New Delhi, UGC, 1990.

India (1988-89); A Reference Annual Ministry of Information and Broadcasting, New Delhi, Publication Division, 1989.

Library Science in Indian Universities – Review Committee Report, New Delhi, UGC, 1965.

Ministry of Human Resources Development – Annual report Pt-I, 1989-90, New Delhi, Deptt. of Education, 1990.

Modern roles of a University Library in improving higher education (Lecture), by A.P. Shrivastava.

National Policy on Education – 1986, Ministry of Human Resource Development, New Delhi, Government of India, 1986.

National Policy for University Libraries in India: Problems and perspectives, Edited by N.B. Inamdar and L.S. Ramaiah, New Delhi, Concept, 1989.

A National Policy and Programme for University Libraries in India, by Desh Pande, K.S. NPULI, New Delhi, Concept, 1989.

Programme of Action: National Policy on Education (1986), Ministry of Human Resources Development, New Delhi, Government of India, 1986.

Review of Social work education in India; retrospect and prospect, 2nd review committee the – Report, New Delhi, UGC, 1980.

Review Committee on the University Grants Commission (1977) – Report, Ministry of Education of Social Welfare, Govt. of India, 1977.

Review Committee on UGC programmes – Report, New Delhi, UGC, 1981.

Role of a Modern University Library, by A.P. Srivastava, Indian Libraries Trends and prospectives.

Survey of the Delhi University Libraries, by Carl M. White, Delhi, University of Delhi, 1965.

Selected Educational Statistics 1988-89, New Delhi, MHRD, 1990.

Speeches of Maulana Azad 1947-1958, New Delhi, Publication Division, 1989.

Standards of University Education – Report New Delhi, UGC, 1965.

The Export Committee on the minimum qualification and workload etc. for librarians and Directors of Physical Education in Universities and Colleges, New Delhi, U.G.C., 1987.

UGC's is Policy and programme for Improvement of Research in the Universities, New Delhi, UGC, 1984.

University Education Commission (1948-49) – Report, Ministry of Education, New Delhi, Govt. of India, 1950.

University Libraries in India, by S.N. Shrivastava and S.C. Verma, New Delhi, Sterling, 1980.

University Libraries of India 1857-1970, by E.G. Viswanathan, New Delhi, 1972.

University Library system in India, by K.S. Deshpande, New Delhi, Sterling, 1985.

University Grants Commission – Annual Report 1988-89, New Delhi, UGC, 1990.

INDEX

CICIL LIST

CONCEPTS IN COMMUNICATION, INFORMATICS & LIBRARIANSHIP

(CICIL)

General Editor: **S.P. AGRAWAL**

CICIL-1 Development of Library Services in India: Social Science Information
S.P. Agrawal Rs. 150

CICIL-2 Development of Documentation in India: Social Science Information
S.P. Agrawal Rs. 250

CICIL-3 UNESCO and Social Sciences: Retrospect and Prospect
S.P. Agrawal and **J.C. Aggarwal** Rs. 250

CICIL-4 INDIANA : A Bibliography of Bibliographical Sources
M.K. Jain Rs. 200

CICIL-5 Dimensions of Library and Information Science: Kaula Festschrift
V. Venkatappaiah (Eds.) Rs. 600

CICIL-6 Book Numbers: Some Indian Methods
M.P. Satija and **S.P. Agrawal** Rs. 100

CICIL-7 National Policy for University Libraries in India: Problems and Perspectives
N.B. Inamdar and **L.S. Ramaiah** (Ed.) Rs. 250

CICIL-8 Media Utilisation for the Development of Women and Children
B.S. Thakur and **Binod C. Agrawal** Rs. 150

CICIL-9 Terrorism: An Annotated Bibliography
Susheela Bhan (Ed.) Rs. 275

CICIL-10 Transnational Library Relations: The Indo-American Experience
M.B. Konnur Rs. 175

CICIL-11 Geography of Marketing and Commercial Activities in India (Documentation on Research Information)
R.S. Dixit Rs. 130

CICIL-12 Information India 1988: Global View
S.P. Agrawal and **J.C. Aggarwal** Rs. 200

CICIL-13 Women's Education in India: Historical Review, Present Status and Perspective Plan
S.P. Agrawal and **J.C. Aggarwal** Rs. 360

CICIL-14 Cultural Communication in India: Role and Impact of Phonograms
J.M. Ojha (in press)

CICIL-15 Second Historical Survey of Educational Development in India: Select Documents 1985-1989
S.P. Agrawal and **J.C. Aggarwal** Rs. 490

CICIL-16 Documentation Encyclopaedia of UNESCO and Education
J.C. Aggarwal and **S.P. Agrawal** Rs. 800 (set of 2 parts)

CICIL-17 Attitude Towards Information: A Study of Post-Graduate Teachers and Researchers in Social Sciences
N.G. Satish (in press)

CICIL-18 Librarianship and Bureaucratic Organisation: A Study in the Sociology of Library Profession in India
P.K. Jayaswal Rs. 175

CICIL-19 Literature Search
K.A. Isaac Rs. 150

CICIL-20 Child Education in India: Index to Scholarly Writings in Indian Educational Journals and Newspapers since independence
S.P. Agrawal and **Naresh Kanta** Rs. 100

CICIL-21 Lok Sabha and Vidhan Sabha Elections in India 1989 & 1990: Process and Results with Comparative Study of Manifestos
S.P. Agrawal and **J.C. Aggarwal** Rs. 250

CICIL-22 Islamic Studies in India: A Survey of Human, Institutional and Documentary Sources
Mohamed Taher Rs. 180

CICIL-23 Panchayati Raj: An Annotated Bibliography
N.B. Inamdar, N.G. Satish and **Anil Takalkar** 290

CICIL-24 Information India 1989-90: Global View
S.P. Agrawal and **J.C. Aggarwal** Rs. 500

CICIL-25 First Handbook of Psychological and Social Instruments
Udai Pareek and **T. Venkateswara Rao** (in press)

CICIL-26 Educational and Social Uplift of Backward Classes: At What Cost and How? Mandal Commission and After
S.P. Agrawal and **J.C. Aggarwal** Rs. 275

CICIL-27 Mass Media and New Horizons: Impact of TV & Video an Urban Milieu **H.R. Trivedi** Rs. 180

CICIL-28 Indian Writings on Education : An Indicator to Indian Educational Journals Grouped by Subject Deseriptors 1979 to 1986 (in two parts) **S.P. Agarwal** Rs. 900 (per set)

CICIL-29 Nation in Crisis
S.P. Agrawal and **J.C. Aggarwal** Rs. 200

CICIL-30 Information India 1990-91: Global View
S.P. Agrawal and **J.C. Aggarwal** Rs. 500

CICIL-31 Development of University Libraries in India After Independence **O.P. Gupta** Rs. 270